Changing Spots

A systems approach to change management

Ian White

Andrew Kearns

Published by Hartswood Press

Publisher address: Hartswood Press, 12 Windsor House, Pynnacles Close, Stanmore, Middx, HA7 4FE

Publisher website: www.hartswoodpress.co.uk

Publisher contact: press@hartswoodmanagement.co.uk

First Published 2017

ISBN: 978-0-9955873-0-4

Contents

Preface

This guide has been prepared by people who have brought about real change in organisations which had previously found change difficult – leopards that needed to change their spots.

The core of the guide describes a systems approach to change management which is effective for organisations that need to make radical change, hence the title "Changing Spots". The focus of this work is to achieve a step change in performance – improvements in competitiveness, financial performance, customer service, quality of conformance, cost effectiveness and employee motivation.

We have called the process of evaluation, design and implementation "Ready, Steady, Change". The methodology involves the use of a "Task Force" of employees who are trained and deployed to change the organisation. Many organisations rightly recognise that their employees are their greatest asset. This methodology embraces and endorses this view, giving it practical expression. Leadership challenges are no more evident than when undertaking major change and this theme is addressed throughout the guide, both at executive and Task Force level.

The first section of the book describes the conditions where such an approach is appropriate and how it might be adapted to meet specific needs.

The next section - Ready Steady Change - describes the change process steps in detail and delivers good practice, leadership advice and practical guidance.

The final section - Reference Material - contains guidance on tools and techniques applicable across the Ready Steady Change methodology and will prove valuable in any type of change project. The areas addressed include benchmarking, process modelling, measures of performance and analysis techniques as well as change methodology.

Much of the methodology and practical experience contained in this guide originates from working practices at Lucas Engineering and Systems a subsidiary of Lucas Industries established in the 1980s. Since then the methodology has been enhanced through application in many business sectors and in public enterprise in the UK and abroad.

Acknowledgements

The inspiration for this guide is the methodology developed under the leadership of Dr John Parnaby CBE (1937 – 2011). The business unit he established within Lucas Industries, Lucas Engineering & Systems (LE&S), achieved a worldwide reputation for delivering manufacturing effectiveness and step change improvement programmes. Building on its successes within Lucas, LE&S helped to transform the competitiveness of many enterprises - including hospitals, food processing plants, and the manufacture of aero engines and automotive components in the UK and abroad.

The staff he recruited, trained and motivated helped develop these concepts. A list of the staff and others involved in step change programs is included in Appendix 1.

Finally the authors would like to thank Jayne Eagles who has helped enormously in providing structure to this guide and Chris Bland for his help with the design and layout.

Introduction

"There is nothing more difficult to take in hand, more perilous to conduct, or more uncertain in its success, than to take the lead in the introduction of a new order of things."

Niccolo Machiavelli (1469-1527) - The Prince (1513)

"It is not necessary to change. Survival is not mandatory."

W. Edwards Deming (1900 – 1993)

"Who needs to change? - - -everyone, but me!"
"Who wants change? - - me, not anyone else!"

Anon

These quotations encapsulate the dilemma for the leader of any organisation. It is vital that the organisation changes but any change will carry a risk of failure and will be resisted. At a strategic level, failure will be visible, expensive and possibly career limiting.

The systems approach to change management, "Ready Steady Change" was developed to assist organisations to make a step change in performance. It can be applied in any organisation and has proved invaluable in many situations, including where there is a history of resistance to change, poor motivation and low morale.

The main elements of the approach are:

"Task Force"

which is established for the purpose of effecting change and will undertake much of the work on behalf of the executive. A Task Force is a multidisciplinary project team of full and part-time members drawn from the business to develop the change proposals required to meet the business need. It is disbanded after its work is completed.

"Ready"

addresses the Senior Executives' responsibility for leadership, as they establish a strategic framework for the organisation, agree the priorities for change and allocate the necessary support and resources.

"Steady"

embraces the detailed work undertaken by the Task Force in developing the specific proposals for change. This is openly communicated in the business and reviewed and approved by the executive.

"Change"

addresses the implementation of agreed proposals, the consolidation of the change and also the deployment of ongoing improvement processes. This is the hardest part, but made easier, and with a higher likelihood of success, when based on the systematic preparation described in the guide.

Many of the ideas in this guide are described elsewhere, but the guide draws them together in a style that can be assimilated at all levels of the organisation. Visual illustrations are used throughout the guide to aid the communication of ideas. Leadership issues are especially critical and are discussed in depth. The Ready Steady Change process is flexible and needs to be tailored to the specific organisation and its situation.

The ideas contained in the guide have now been successfully applied in hundreds of organisations, in the private sector (manufacturing, distribution, banking, utilities), central and local government and publically owned enterprises. The results are dramatic, both in the improvement of measurable business performance and in the impact on employee motivation and the organisation's flexibility. Many of the early adopting manufacturing businesses are now world class.

Section 1

Is the approach for me and my organisation?

The systems approach to radical change appears straightforward, but before addressing the methodology in detail, there are key questions for the reader to address:

• Has the organisation been successful in implementing major change in the past?

• What kind of change is the organisation planning and how difficult will it be?

• Is a change methodology needed?

• Will I need to adapt my leadership style?

• How much time and resource will "Ready Steady Change" require?

These questions will also need to be addressed by colleagues in the Leadership Team.

Has the organisation been successful in implementing major change in the past?

This is not always an easy question to address. The Leadership Team may have differing views on the success or failure of past strategic plans and change initiatives.

It may help to position the organisation in a "Change Manager's" matrix. This sets out the need for change in one dimension and the capacity or capability of the organisation to make change in the other. This is a subjective assessment, but it provides a starting point for discussion with colleagues.

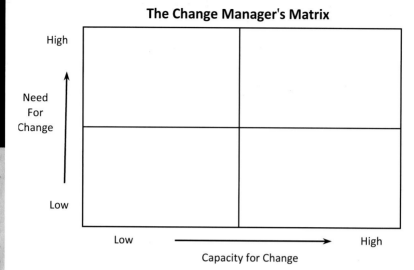

The need for change, business priorities and the required pace of change should have emerged from a strategic review. A high need for change usually reflects an intensely competitive environment. Symptoms of a high need for change include:

- Rapidly changing technology, products or market dynamics.

- Reducing market share.

- Reducing profitability.

- Ageing product portfolio.

- Negative customer feedback or failure to win new contracts.

An organisation's capacity for change will reflect the attitudes, capabilities and the past experience of its employees.

- Low capacity for change is often seen in organisations that have high absenteeism and where staff have low morale. Staff are often job focussed and with an inflexible "not my job" culture. Internal communication is often poor.

• High capacity for change is found in organisations that are small or structured in process based teams; staff are flexible and not status conscious. They feel valued for their contribution to the organisation rather than for the job to which they are currently assigned. They will have been trained in improvement techniques and communication will be two way and open. There will be a strong focus on customer service.

These additional questions may be helpful to assess your organisation's capacity for change.

• Is there recent experience of implementing large change projects? Were they successful and to schedule?

• Do staff change job roles /assignments regularly? Are they encouraged to be flexible?

• Do improvement groups operate throughout the business and produce visible results?

• How does the organisation recognise improvements that are generated by staff? How many ideas are generated in a year and how many are implemented?

• Do the communication methods of the organisation create an open culture or is communication limited or one way?

• Will staff volunteer to lead projects?

The four quadrants of the matrix are sometimes given labels:

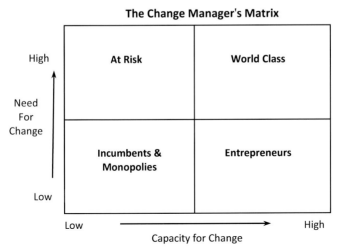

The Change Manager's Matrix

	At Risk	**World Class**
	Incumbents & Monopolies	**Entrepreneurs**

High / Low — Need For Change

Low ——→ High — Capacity for Change

There is a broad spectrum within each quadrant of the matrix:

• World Class: Leading international manufacturing businesses in fiercely competitive markets e.g. automotive, information technology, pharmaceuticals, etc.

• Entrepreneurs: Usually small rapidly growing organisations that rely on strong patents, innovation and niche markets for their initial success. Established entrepreneurial organisations will eventually face increasing competition and will need to aim for the world-class quadrant.

• At Risk: Organisations that operate in competitive markets but are reliant on customer inertia, low wages, or high barriers to market entry for their continued independence.

• Incumbents and Monopolies: Continue to exist as a result of largely protected positions and lack of consumer choice or viable competition. These include can Local Authorities and publically owned enterprises. Of course performance varies within this quadrant. Many publically owned enterprises are concerned about their performance, budget constraints, reputation, regulators or the prospect of privatisation and out-sourcing, and so face a high need for change.

Each organisation must assess for itself where it lies in the matrix.

The value of the matrix is not that of an analytical tool. Rather it can be used by the Leadership Team to develop an aligned view and provide a simple visual communication of the need for the organisation to improve.

In the private sector, most businesses are seeking to maintain or improve their competitive position but are not necessarily achieving the improvements that will make this happen.

The leadership challenge is to make a realistic judgement of the need for change and the capacity for change

For the organisation

For its main competitors

and to position these in the matrix. "Changing Spots" and the Ready Steady Change methodology is targeted at organisations who need to increase their capacity for change.

What kind of change is the organisation planning and how difficult will it be?

Strategic plans may involve investment in new technology, markets and new products. They may require business acquisitions, mergers, divestments, new business or manufacturing processes, business resizing, closure or transfer of work to low cost regions. The options are unlimited and large organisations will be considering several simultaneous changes.

All could be critical to the success of the enterprise and all could prove irrelevant, if a critical external competitive opportunity or threat is missed or ignored. The Internet is an obvious example of a technology change that has been vital for some and fatal for others.

The priority of competing opportunities and the state of the competition start to give us a view of the "need" for change. The process of identifying strategic opportunities is not the focus of this guide and is well covered elsewhere, however, the implementation of strategy, i.e. "the How to Change" is central to the guide.

Anyone with experience of managing staff in an organisation will recognise that everyone is very sensitive to the suggestion that any change is being planned. Leaders know from experience that some types of change will be much more difficult than others.

The "Difficulty Ladder" illustrates some types of change. They are classified as Operational and Strategic and the sequence of increasing difficulty is based on practical experience.

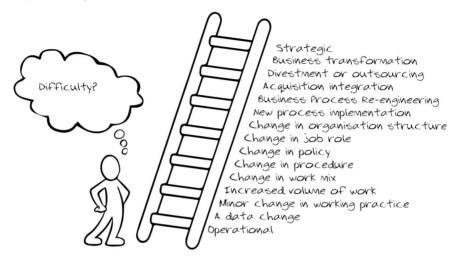

The exact sequence can be debated but changes which threaten loss of jobs are always near the top, closely followed by changes to terms and conditions of employment and job role due to the direct impact on employees. Strategic initiatives will involve major change and may threaten employees' feeling of security.

Although operational change is usually achieved with less resistance, it too has the potential to cause chaos and confusion, impacting customer service.

Any change can trigger unrest and reduce morale. In addition, there is often an unspoken concern that the employee will not be able to cope in the new situation. They may have worked in the same role for many years and may feel they have skill inadequacies or fear the use of new technologies. One of the leadership challenges is to adopt a change methodology that will increase support and commitment among employees for the proposals. The Ready Steady Change methodology is especially effective for the most difficult types of change.

Is a change methodology needed? (Isn't it just a project plan by another name?)

The first leadership challenge is to ensure that the organisation's strategic priorities are well chosen. The second is to ensure that they are well implemented.

The choice of "How" to bring about strategic change can be confusing and depends on a number of factors; in particular the scale and pace of change that is necessary and the degree of difficulty anticipated.

Does the organisation require step change --- as well as continuous improvement?

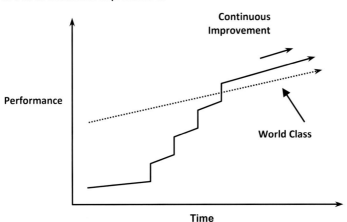

17

There is no single right path to successful implementation and there is a risk that the responsibility for implementation will be delegated to project or line managers without the options being properly considered. Leaders dictating outcomes without being clear about the process are not demonstrating leadership.

If executives are uncertain in their choice of how to manage major change, then that leadership issue should be addressed head on. This is part of the purpose of this guide. Without an agreed methodology, the organisation's efforts will not be integrated and aligned.

Most of us fear the unknown and the methodology should address this issue at the outset. At a very basic level, many employees perceive any significant change to their environment as a threat. A few may see it as an opportunity.

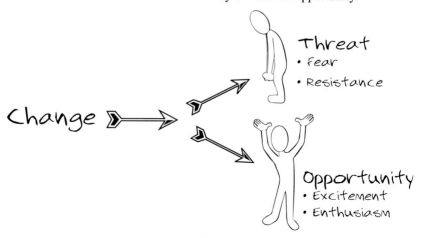

If the majority of staff in the organisation are "above the line", the introduction of any change will be difficult. Any problems will be met with "It'll never work", "I told you so" and "It didn't work last time we tried". In these circumstances the results may not meet expectations and the organisation may drift back to old ways of working.

The model below illustrates some of the key features that can reduce the level of fear, resistance to change and their close cousin, apathy.

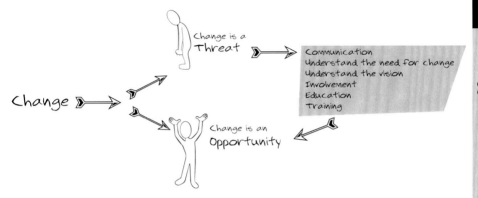

In almost every strategic change situation, the support or, at least, the understanding of staff will make the change process easier and more certain. A change methodology should include a systematic way of getting staff "on board"- moving them from seeing the change as a threat to seeing it as an opportunity.

Key steps for the Leadership Team are:

• Create an understanding that the organisation needs to change (to survive, to compete, to grow, to meet customer demands, to meet the demands of "the Regulator", to cope with cuts in funding, etc.).

• Communicate the vision (where is the organisation going, how will it get there, what timescales).

• Provide an opportunity for involvement in the process (ideally as contributor, but at least through being asked for comments, views and suggestions).

• Deliver education so that employees can understand the ideas and methodology behind the change.

• Plan the training that will be essential for all those who are asked to change their role or methods of working. In the early stages it is important to reassure employees that full training will be given.

The Ready Steady Change methodology addresses all of these issues by focussing on the what and how of delivering improvement.

Will I need to adapt my leadership style?

Four aspects of leadership style will become critical in transforming the business. Leadership Teams who follow the Ready Steady Change approach will need to adopt or adapt their style.

1. Be prepared to take a holistic view

The iceberg is a good metaphor for an organisation. The Leadership Team can directly influence the parts above the waterline.

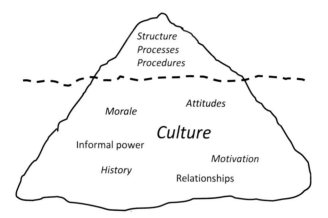

The parts of the organisation "below the waterline" cannot be influenced so easily. However, they need to be recognised, understood and taken into account in planning a change programme:

• Structure – The organisation structure, management responsibilities, job definitions, job grades, job roles and the way in which the activities are allocated to teams and how the teams are managed.

• Processes – the basic activities by which the organisation turns its inputs into value added outputs for its customers, together with the processes that support these value-added activities and the performance measures by which success is judged.

• Procedures (including the IT systems) – the written and coded descriptions, training material and mechanisms by which the processes are undertaken.

• Culture – the way in which the values of individuals and the organisation are expressed. The Culture is a complex mix of a number of elements which are often intangible and include the attitude of staff to the organisation they work for, to their peers and their customers. The mix also includes staff morale, self-confidence, feeling of well-being and staff motivation to achieve objectives and improve the operation of the organisation.

Chief executives asked to describe their organisation will be confident to talk about the products, markets and customers. They will be able to describe the organisation structure and roles and responsibilities and will be familiar with the main processes, policies and procedures that staff follow. Like an iceberg, these are the parts of an organisation that lie "above the water line". However, they may struggle to describe what lies below the surface.

It is not uncommon for a new chief executive to make changes to the organisation structure. Once decided, such changes can be imposed and implemented relatively quickly. Changes to processes and procedures take longer. They need to be accompanied by design, documentation, training and trialling before implementation. In a haste to "make a difference", chief executives have been known to ignore the impact of structural change (and the associated changes in roles and responsibilities) on business processes.

Like the iceberg, the culture of the organisation lies below the waterline. The culture will change but changes can be positive or negative, and positive changes are hard to win and cannot be imposed.

Leaders need to take time to develop a view of the existing culture and whether it is homogeneous. Also, a new leader might ask what changes in culture would enhance the organisation's competitiveness, increase flexibility and internal co-operation or improve customer service. Current and desired organisational values are often a place to start.

My attitudes are my own

Planning to change the organisation is like planning to move the iceberg. The whole iceberg needs to be moved. The Leadership Team could demand a change to the organisation's structure and processes; it can only seek a change in culture.

A successful leader will recognise that a shared awareness of the desired culture will assist the design of the structure and processes whilst the choice of organisation structure, team design and process options will impact on the culture. Their design needs to be considered together. This is an example of thinking holistically.

2. Lead people through change - Understand the trauma that change can bring.

If we can see the impact of change from the viewpoint of our staff, we will be better equipped to manage the process. Changes that we see as relatively minor can be viewed very differently by those directly involved.

The Transition Curve*, first published by Elisabeth Kübler-Ross, illustrates the reaction of people to shock or changed circumstances.

These can be domestic or work related and range from the most severe, e.g. death of a spouse or child, through to relatively inconsequential changes. Work related change can be high on the list with issues like "potential loss of job" and "loss of status", whilst apparently positive changes like "promotion" can also cause concerns and drive negative feelings.

The sequence of reactions is predictable:

- Anxiety, fear, shock and/or immobilisation

- Denial of change

- Feeling of depression or lack of self-worth

- Acceptance of the new situation

- Growth in confidence

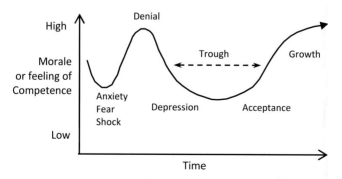

*Source:
Kübler-Ross, E. (2005) *On Grief and Grieving: Finding the Meaning of Grief Through the Five Stages of Loss*, Simon & Schuster Ltd, <u>ISBN 0-7432-6344-8</u>

A leader who understands that this represents a normal pattern of human reaction is better placed to ensure that the change is planned in a way which will minimise the impact.

In a business context, the initial "shock" of an announcement will be modified by the way the message is presented and the opportunity for staff to have their initial fears and concerns addressed. Although loss of morale may be inevitable, the depth and duration of the trough can be influenced. At the simplest level, staff who are given reassurance and full training will recover faster than those who aren't.

It is a leader's responsibility to understand these reactions and to take account of them when planning communications, workshops and Task Force activities in order to minimise the impact of change on the individual.

A further more detailed discussion of the Transition Curve is contained in Section 3 Reference Material - The Transition Curve.

3. Communicate openly

For the Ready Steady Change process to be effective, leaders must be prepared to be entirely open in respect of the change programme. This openness should also apply to the style of Task Force and project communication.

Although most organisations strive for good communications with employees, an open style may be lost when it comes to strategic change issues. Real issues of commercial confidentiality can intervene as well as the personal style of some leaders to "tell people only what they need to know". These issues need to be addressed for successful implementation since staff will not commit to change if they believe leaders are not being open.

Leaders can dramatically improve the experience of change for their staff by the way in which they, and their management team, communicate. It needs to be the right communication, at the right time, in the right way. Too often communication is based on e-mail, the notice board or on an annual presentation. There may be an opportunity for questions but, in reality, few people put their head above the parapet. There is no discussion and little mutual understanding.

Good practice in communication is a theme of the guide but leaders will appreciate that the trigger for a change programme in an organisation is often bad news. The change programme itself can result in bad news as well as good. One person's cost reduction can be another's job loss.

Good or bad news, the maxim "No secrets, no surprises" should apply for leaders and Task Forces alike. This degree of openness may not appeal to or may not fit with the organisation's existing culture.

4. Give up control to gain control - let others do the detail

Strategic change is difficult and time consuming and the analysis, design and implementation are well beyond the scope of any individual. To be successful the leader needs to delegate control over the detail of the solution and its implementation whilst retaining control over the leadership process by which change will be approved and authorised. The Task Force provides the best vehicle to achieve this aim.

Task Forces need to include members from a range of functions and skill levels. Team Leaders and professional staff also have a role and other members may include employee or trade union representatives.

In some situations, customers and suppliers have participated in the work of the Task Force. Staff at all levels have a real contribution to make. They are aware of the detail and will also be able to anticipate implementation problems. Involving them at an early stage will help their personal development and equip them to be able to communicate the ideas to their peers.

> The power of involving people in the change process:
>
> "Change done to us – is a threat.
> Change done by us - is fun."
>
> This was generated by a group of staff in an aerospace business that had been empowered to double the sales per employee, reduce lead-times by 75% and enhance customer service.

These four aspects of leadership style are important to the methodology. The Leadership Team need to decide whether they can embrace them and how they can demonstrate leadership of change.

How much time and resource will "Ready Steady Change" require?

The answer depends on the project to be addressed but, as guide, a process redesign Task Force for an office based activity could take 2-3 months to prepare and agree a concept design and a further 2-4 months for detail design and implementation support. The following are pointers for the resource required:

- A Task Force works best with a core of 3 to 7 full time members who may be involved for up to a year for a complex redesign.

- The effort to establish and train a Task Force can be considerable. Members of the Leadership Team can do much of the training and it will help them develop their own skills.

- External facilitation of workshops and Task Force training will be an advantage.

This level of resource puts the approach beyond many very small organisations. However, there are alternatives e.g. conventional project teams using the methodology, directed improvement groups and part-time Task Forces, particularly when supporting Leadership Team initiatives.

Summary

The Ready Steady Change approach can be useful in the implementation of strategic plans, and can also be adapted to assist in many others. The following table highlights some common organisation changes that a Leadership Team might regard as strategic and an initial view of whether Ready Steady Change might be of benefit.

25

Strategic Opportunity	Is Ready Steady Change appropriate?
Business Acquisition and Mergers	Task Forces can be used to help integrate the organisations by addressing synergy, performance and cultural issues. They can develop forward plans and improve morale.
Lean processes and process redesign	Ideally suited. A Multi-disciplinary Task Force gives fantastic results by developing detailed process improvements.
Changes in behaviour, culture and attitude	The focus on involvement makes this approach one of the best vehicles available.
Cost reduction, rightsizing, downsizing	Can be effective, particularly if time is available to tackle issues systematically. Gives a powerful alternative to the more traditional approach of "20% off each department's budget in 2 months"
Consolidation and relocation	Can be used to develop forward plans, transfer skills and to maintain or build morale.
Divestments and outsourcing	Can be useful to maintain value and quality as well as employee relationships and morale
New product technology	The principles can be vital to ensure that marketing, design and production work together.
Establish new markets	Possibly not relevant.

Not all organisations are trying to "change their spots" but many leaders want to make significant change by empowering their employees. Using the "Ready Steady Change" methodology will enhance the implementation of most change programmes.

Section 2

Ready Steady Change

Throughout this section we will focus on both the process of bringing about step change as well as the leadership issues which can arise.

For convenience and simplicity of presentation, the methodology is described in three stages. In this it is analogous to "ready-aim-fire" or "ready-steady-go".

In a major change programme there is often overlap between the 3 stages with interaction between them, however this structure should assist the reader in planning their own approach.

We will take each stage in turn, looking for good practice and examples to illustrate the process.

In each of these stages a number of steps will be described, starting in each case with the particular leadership issues to be addressed.

Ready

The topics addressed within the Ready phase are highlighted below, starting with leadership:

Ready → **Leadership**
   Build "Need for Change"
   Create Vision
   Establish Route Map
   Commit Resource
   Communication

The leadership challenge for the Sponsor of a major change programme is to ensure that leadership colleagues support the venture. A series of "one on one" discussions with colleagues is probably the best way to establish the level of support, commitment and enthusiasm which can be expected. Here are some questions for discussion:

- Is there a shared view of "the need for change"?

- Is there a shared vision for the organisation?

- Is there a shared view of how to get there?

- Who should take responsibility for making change happen?

- Is there a shared view of priorities?

Let us take the first question as an example: "Is there a shared view of the need for change?"

In private enterprise, leaders normally feel the pressure of competition and often get direct feedback from customers, financiers and shareholders. They will feel a collective need for change, though not necessarily in their own function or specialism.

In "non-competitive" organisations, leadership colleagues may be ignorant or unconcerned about the real drivers of change in the organisation, as they may not impact their function.

Individual discussions with colleagues should be enough to assess their understanding of and their support for a change initiative. Will they help or hinder change?

Those discussions usually provide the best way to assess a colleague's thinking and potential personal support. Initial discussions are likely to focus on the questions around the need for change and the vision for the organisation. The support of leadership colleagues is so essential to success that proceeding without their support will be, at best, risky.

The next step in the approach is to establish a "shared view" of the need for change, vision and methodology. An executive workshop process has proven to be the best way to achieve this common mind. This topic will be addressed again shortly and there is also further information in Section 3 Reference Material – Planning a workshop.

Before proceeding, it's also useful to consider the potential support at other levels of the organisation where the response may be very different.

Middle managers are often the engine room of the organisation and focus on getting the business done. They are often loyal but they are accustomed to being in control and will defend their turf. Some may be very ambitious. Major change may present threats and challenges and, although this group will seldom oppose change overtly, they can represent a serious challenge by undermining the efforts of others.

The staff reaction will vary according to the past record of the organisation in introducing change but, almost by definition, if the capacity for change in the business is judged to be low, then most staff will see proposals as a threat and react accordingly. There is work to do to identify and nurture the resources that will give us the energy to change.

Good change leadership will address the needs of all of these groups and the starting point is the executive team.

Ready → Leadership
Build "need for change"
Create Vision
Establish Route Map
Commit Resource
Communication

Building an agreed "need for change" is critical so that staff and leadership in an organisation can take the next step. It is this "need for change" that will demonstrate that the change is not "change for change's sake". Often a "Trigger Event" (such as a dramatic loss of customer confidence or the loss of a major order) provides the impetus for change, however, in the "worst-case" scenario, many of the executive group may not yet see an organisation wide need for change. Those that do support the change may feel that change is needed, but in another department:

> "If only production delivered on time, we would be able to increase market share" or "If procurement had got the goods on the shelf, we would have made our forecast."

This type of debate is circular; it seldom results in either the identification of root causes of problems or the development of effective change programmes. Benchmarking should be used to break this cycle.

The organisation needs to establish that it is possible to operate in a dramatically more effective way. Comparisons with competitive organisations are the most obvious way of seeking benchmark data. In the 1980s, UK based automotive component manufacturers were able to make the comparision that Japanese competitors could operate with 50% fewer indirect staff and with product defect levels measured in parts per million.

Comparisons with non-competitive organisations can also provide insights into best practice. The comparisons can include the business processes which are critical for competitiveness e.g. product development, sales, operations, distribution, warehousing, logistics, HR, financial control etc.

Customer feedback provides a valuable source of information that may help clarify the need for change.

Ready - Build "need for change"

Ready - Build "need for change"

The CEO of a repair and overhaul business had been led to believe that a 10% price reduction was the only way to dent the competition. A customer survey using trade-off analysis showed that a price reduction would help (it always does), but the main order qualifying criteria was reliably meeting quoted repair dates, and the winning criteria was a reduction in repair lead time by an eye watering 75%. This became the target for the transformation project, rather than a 10% price reduction which the competitors could have easily copied, to everyone's detriment.

Leaders often build the organisation's "need for change" based on external drivers e.g. customer service or competitiveness. These will engage and motivate staff behind a common purpose. Internal drivers (e.g. cost reduction or profit improvement) may cause division rather than motivate staff. A target to increase "sales per employee by 35%" may require staff redundancies and a target to reduce costs by 35% almost certainly will.

Most organisations set aside a budget for management training and development and some of that might usefully fund benchmarking studies. There is further detailed information in Section 3 Reference Material - Benchmarking the organisation and Customer feedback.

One of the most effective ways of airing "need for change" material and gaining a shared commitment to a change programme is to run an executive workshop. However, it is well to remember that up front "one to one" discussions with all of those who will be present, as described earlier, will increase the chances of success, and forewarn of problems. One on one discussion in advance also demonstrates the maxim "NO SECRETS, NO SURPRISES!"

An Input / Output diagram highlights the main features of an executive workshop that has been established to develop the leadership's shared support for a change programme:

Inputs	Executive Workshop	Outputs
Business Strategy	Objectives agreed	Leadership
Benchmark information	Need for change agreed	Agreed need for change
Training	Priorities agreed	Change strategy
Change methodology	Vision Developed	Vision
External input	Plan outlined	Priorities
Workshop Program	Resources committed	Term of reference
Facilitator		Objectives
		Resources
		Task Force

A workshop is not a training programme although it will provide some training. It is a working session which will allow the team to develop, refine and document their plans. Inputs might include:

- A review of business strategy or that part of it which is relevant to the change programme.

- A summary of benchmark information that has been assembled.

- Training input in basic analysis techniques (e.g. Brainstorming, Input-output analysis and SWOT) to allow some team-based syndicate work. There is a detailed description of these techniques in Section 3 Reference Material.

- A review of the proposed change methodology including an introduction to the Task Force approach as a basis for step change.

- External input e.g. from a customer, university or supplier.

- A facilitator for the process, either sourced externally or an uninvolved but politically aware senior manager.

Time will be scheduled for the Leadership Team to work through the steps needed to address each of the questions. A key feature of an executive workshop is that the facilitator should not allow the process to "move on" until there has been a shared agreement to each stage.

The questions to address are the same for most organisations:

"Have we agreed the objectives of the workshop?"

"Have we agreed the need for change?"

"Quantified?"

"Have we agreed a vision of how the organisation will look?"

"Have we agreed the priorities for a change programme and the objectives we will set?"

"Have we agreed the resource required and that we will take steps to make them available?"

"Have we agreed the next steps including how the results of this workshop will be communicated?"

Planning and running workshops Section 3 Reference Material - Planning a workshop.

33

Ready → Leadership
     Build "need for change"
     Create Vision
     Establish Route Map
     Commit Resource
     Communication

The greatest fear for most employees is "fear of the unknown". Creating a shared vision for the organisation can help reduce barriers to change. Leaders need to ensure that the organisation shares a vision of the future.

It has been said, "If we don't know where we are going, any road will do!"

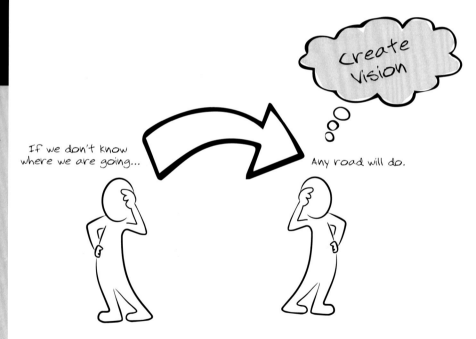

The Vision should be an inspiration to all staff and, if it is visual, pictorial and easy to assimilate, so much the better. It should describe what the future could, and should, be like and build on the need for change. It should seem like a significant stretch but not far-fetched. The Leadership Team should take time to develop a vision aligning external (market) achievements and performance improvement that can be used throughout the programme. The vision statements of some organisations illustrate the need for change, initial priorities, quantified targets, the process for change (e.g. Task Forces, problem-solving etc.), resources and time plan.

The vision may include a route map which shows practical steps on the journey. A popular template is shown below:

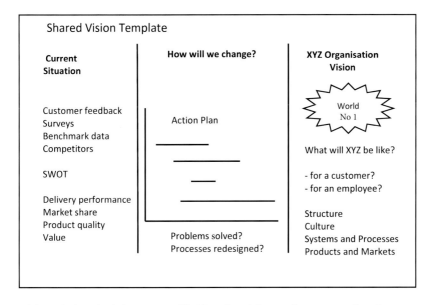

This style has the advantage of linking the vision to the current situation. An actual example generated by an executive team contains fairly specific information about what they plan to achieve:

35

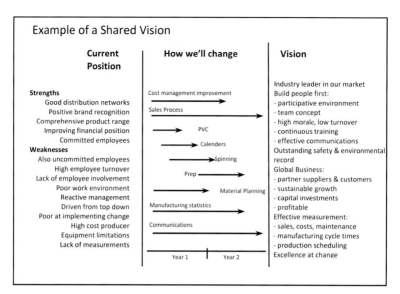

Example of a Shared Vision

Current Position	How we'll change	Vision

In the above case the vision was conceived by the executive and developed and refined by the management group and the Task Force over a period of two weeks.

There are no rights or wrongs in this, but the management team and the workforce need to commit to the vision.

Ready → Leadership
    Build "need for change"
    Create Vision
    Establish Route Map
    Commit Resource
    Communication

The Leadership Team needs to prepare the route map or programme of projects.

The route map should be prepared based on the business strategy and the agreements at the workshop. The route map may need to include a concept design. A concept design describes the anticipated future shape of the organisation i.e. the outcome of the successful improvement programme. Like a blueprint, it shows the outline of what things will be like rather than the full detail, which will be developed later.

There are two approaches to developing a concept design. In the first, the design is arrived at top down by the Leadership Team. In the second a Task Force is appointed to do the work. The strengths and weaknesses of the two approaches are shown in the following table:

Approach	Key strengths	Key weaknesses
Leadership Team develop Concept Design	Can be quick and focussed. Does not create uncertainty because it is not visible to the organisation.	Depends on knowledge and data being available to the leadership team. It can appear like an executive team "stitch up" when it is announced.
Task Force develop Concept Design	Thorough approach using knowledgeable staff in the organisation. Creates the opportunity for an early involvement for team members in the redesign programme.	Requires early communication that will need careful management. Requires a Task Force of strong and committed individuals and a good relationship with the executive team.

One organisation used this illustration to show the relationship between the Leadership Team and the Task Force during concept design:

It is important that there is a strong partnership between the Executive team and the Task Force developing the concept design.

The Task Force should be given responsibility for developing a proposed concept design and the route map (i.e. outline plan, outline business case and proposed programme management structure).

The route map should answer the following questions:

- Is the programme viable?

- What will it cover and when?

- How will it be managed?

- What resources (e.g. people, finances) will it require?

The deliverables making up the route map are:

1. Concept design - A concept design describes the anticipated future shape of the organisation.

(Information can be found in Section 3 Reference Material - Developing a concept design)

2. Outline Business Case – the benefits and costs of the programme.

3. Programme Plan – the overall timeline (including key milestones) and the resources.

4. Project Briefs, sometimes called "Terms of Reference". At this stage, these may be outline statements of what needs to be done and who is responsible for each separate improvement project. The project brief, project scope and objectives need to be confirmed by the Sponsor before the Project Launch.

5. Programme Organisation including responsibilities (the owner and programme manager) and management structures (e.g. steering meetings and reviews).

All these elements should be agreed by the full Leadership Team before moving on in to the Steady stage. With a fair wind this may be possible in the first workshop but, if necessary, use a second workshop or leadership meeting to get sign off. The Executive Team should review these deliverables, amending and finalising them and providing feedback in a constructive manner to maintain the motivation of the Task Force.

Ready → Leadership
      Build "need for change"
      Create Vision
      Establish Route Map
      Commit Resource
      Communication

The Leadership Team needs to demonstrate support for the methodology and the change programme. The financial implications of the programme should be covered in the business case and the project budget but the real test of commitment is to reach agreement on the appointment of the right staff to the programme.

Key Roles in Ready Steady Change Methodology - these roles are required as part of managing a properly established change programme:

> Steering Group - usually drawn from the Leadership Team. Responsible for committing resources, shaping design and supporting implementation.

> Sponsor - the director / manager who oversees the project. This is a part-time but time consuming role. The sponsor is not a Task Force member.

> Task Force Leader - a capable manager who is respected by both managers and staff. Motivated and with the drive to deliver transformational change. Must be full-time. Someone you can not afford to lose to the team.

> Task Force Full-time members - a core team from the range of disciplines and knowledge needed to develop the design proposals and support implementation. They must be full-time and drawn from all levels of the organisation. Include an employee representative and consider volunteers.

> Task Force Part-time members – to provide specialist input and act as a gateway into those functions that do not need full-time involvement.

Most members of the Leadership Team will be required to participate in the steering of the project, helping with resource issues, communications and in providing ready access to their functions.

The Project Sponsor will probably be a member of the Leadership Team. The Sponsor may change for different parts of the programme. Although not full-time, the Sponsor's role will require excellent leadership skills, time and energy.

The Task Force Leader for the first project is a critical appointment. Candidates should be selected early in the process. In some cases, they have been identified before the change programme has been finalised and will be

Ready - Commit Resource

able to attend and participate in executive workshops.

Some common characteristics of Task Force Leaders:

- Known and respected by leaders, colleagues and employees.

- Good understanding of the organisation where change is required.

- Upwardly mobile; this assignment will be a valuable part of their personal development.

- Able to combine strong project and team management capabilities.

The Task Force Leader will need to be released from their current role for a period of 6 to 12 months and changes to provide cover or a replacement will be part of this decision. A successful Task Force Leader is likely to have a role in managing the changed area post implementation.

The decision to deploy operations staff on a full time basis to a Task Force for a number of months is a challenge for any size of enterprise. However, it is a challenge, which cannot be avoided. Part-time improvement groups have their place in bringing about change, but they lack the capacity, commitment and scale to bring about transformational change. The appointment of Task Force core and part-time members will be confirmed during the Steady phase.

A Task Force should consist of a minimum of three and a maximum of eight full time members, depending on the work to be done. The overall composition of the team should reflect:

- Knowledge of the working of the areas being changed.

- Mix of ages and years of experience in the company.

- Mix of team roles (some organisations use psychometric testing to establish effective teams e.g. "Belbin" or "Myers Briggs" assessments. These can be very useful in team selection and team building if they are professionally administered).

- Technical knowledge (e.g. engineering, IT, purchasing /procurement) appropriate to the change.

It is useful to agree 2 or 3 part-time team members. Their primary role is to provide easy access to their function, to assist Task Force communication and to provide particular specialist knowledge. They will participate in the training and development of the project plan.

The Task Force Leader, with guidance from the Sponsor, should make the final selection of team members. Many organisations request volunteers, though it is important to use a clear process for selection if you follow this route. Select people who work well in teams and consider using personality profiling to help with the selection process. Include some people who will bring the change methodology to the team and coach the other team members. One option is to delay final team selection until after Task Force training; this allows staff an opportunity to confirm that they want to be involved and for the Task Force Leader to see them work together.

The organisation's operational performance must be maintained throughout the change process despite the allocation of resources to the Task Force. Responsibilities may be passed completely to existing staff, divided between a manager and a colleague or interim staff brought in to backfill the roles. There needs to be a clear role for each individual at the conclusion of the Task Force assignment. If these issues are not resolved, team members will carry their operational responsibilities in to the project and underperform in both activities.

It is critical to ensure that agreement to these resourcing decisions is underwritten by the leadership team.

Ready → Leadership
Build "need for change"
Create Vision
Establish Route Map
Commit Resource
Communication

There have been many studies that review the effectiveness of communications in organisations. With few exceptions, people prefer to be given important information directly by their boss in an environment where they can ask questions. Change programmes will affect staff in many different ways but excellent communication will always lead to a better outcome.

The principle content of communications during the Ready phase will include:

- The Need for Change - why change is necessary.

- The Vision statement - the aim of the change.

- The Concept Design - the outcome in outline.

- The Route Map - how the work is to be undertaken.

- Next Steps.

Should all the elements be delivered in one presentation? This depends on the circumstances. If the programme is going to be painful (e.g. cost savings and redundancies) it is critical that the Need for Change is carefully explained. However this presentation should describe enough of the Route Map so that the staff understand what the next steps are. In general, information about the project/programme should be provided to the staff as it is developed.

Many types of communication and presentation media are available and most organisations have an established style.

Ready - Communication

Presentations to small groups work well because of the opportunity to ask questions. If the group size is greater than 20, the proportion of people asking questions reduces dramatically. The executive team member responsible for those involved should lead these early presentations. If the organisation is too large to do this effectively, then the presentation should be given to the management team to cascade to their staff. It should be based on a briefing note that can subsequently be posted on notice boards, e-mailed etc.

Summary of good practice in communication presentations:

- Manager-led but use a number of presenters (this helps reinforce the "shared view" and give presentation practice to more inexperienced team members).

- Use visuals and pictures.

- Always include a time for questions.

- Encourage questions (and leave a significant silence).

- Prepare for the question time – listeners will be asking what the change means for them.

- Keep a record of questions and replies.

If the organisation is not used to these types of presentations then it may take some time for the staff to get used to the question time.

A Final check

The importance of leadership has been emphasised often during this phase. A change programme will generate resistance, the key questions are:

- Where will it come from?

- How much?

- Can the resistance be countered or harnessed?

It will be important to consider these questions before the first Task Force is launched.

There are two techniques which can assist the Sponsor by providing a structured framework, help test progress and flush out additional issues:

Force Field Analysis

Key Relationship Mapping

Force Field Analysis is used to look at the organisation as a whole. This analysis involves identifying key forces driving and resisting the change project. A plan of action to increase support and reduce resistance is developed.

Key relationship mapping looks at the change from the perspective of key individuals who have organisational power or influence. This too leads to a plan of action.

Information is provided on both techniques in Section 3 Reference Material – Looking for Road Blocks. Force Field Analysis will be useful to the Task Force as they plan implementation.

Conclusion

If all has gone well, you have support from your colleagues, agreed priorities, agreement to the idea of using a Task Force and a commitment to provide resources.

You are
READY.
Well
done!

Steady

The Steady phase focuses on the use of a Task Force to develop the change proposals. The guide will describe the role of the Project Sponsor, the selection and training of the Task Force and the methodology proposed for a typical change project. Again Section 3 Reference Material contains support material that will provide further detail in the use of specific tools and techniques.

Steady → **Leadership**
        Programme management
        Task Force training workshop and project launch
        Project planning
        Using standards
        Producing the design proposal
        Planning implementation
        Task Force communication

Entering the Steady phase presents more leadership challenges. The Project Sponsor should ensure that colleagues remain on board and that they fulfil their commitments. This can be checked during steering group meetings and confirmed by including the change programme updates in Leadership meetings.

As a member of the Leadership Team, the Sponsor needs to ensure that the change programme continues to be aligned to the goals and objectives of the organisation.

The Sponsor also has the direct responsibility for the Task Force Leader and the team. Critically this includes their training and morale at a stage when the team will be taking personal and professional risks. Sponsors need to demonstrate, by their actions, a belief in the core values that will sustain the change programme through inevitable difficulties, promptly resolving issues as they arise.

Other responsibilities include:

- Avoiding the temptation to "do the work" themselves.

- Being on hand to provide guidance.

- Understanding the methodology and ensuring that the Task Force use it effectively.

- Being open in communication with the Task Force and the staff.

- Ensuring that plans (including communication plans) are developed and delivered.

- Providing reassurance that the buck stops with the Sponsor and the Leadership Team.

Task Force Leaders will also face challenges, no less onerous, and of which they may have little experience. Initial leadership challenges for the Task Force Leader include:

- Helping select the team.

- Establishing credibility with the team.

- Establishing a team culture (work ethic, supportive attitude, "can do" approach, enthusiasm) which may not be evident in the rest of the organisation.

- Demonstrating the same beliefs and core values as the Sponsor.

It is a daunting list but it is remarkable how Task Force Leaders rise to the challenge. The Sponsor needs to be the coach, mentor and guardian of the Task Force Leader.

Steady → Leadership
Programme management
Task Force training workshop and project launch
Project planning
Using standards
Producing the design proposal
Planning implementation
Task Force communication

The Steady stage focuses on a single transformation project. In practice the organisation might be running multiple transformation projects in parallel - a change programme. Each project should be set up in the same way, but if these projects as a whole group are expected to deliver additional benefits then it would be wise to run them as a single transformation programme, particularly if:

- There is a cost reason for doing so e.g. there are shared resources (both people and finance).

- There is an opportunity to be realised e.g. enhanced benefits, by aligning the projects. The potential benefits may be intangible e.g. faster development of change capabilities.

An extensive programme will require a full-time Programme Manager and there will be additional reporting and co-ordination requirements. It is the responsibility of the Sponsor to ensure that the Change Programme is kept on track.

Project reviews need to address: scope, quality, time and cost, benefits, quick wins and risk. The Sponsor should plan the following review methods for each project:

- Informal but timetabled weekly review meeting with the Task Force.

- Informal discussions with the Task Force Leader.

- Formal reviews with the Steering Group either monthly or at major milestones. The Leadership Team will need updates of progress and opportunities to shape critical recommendations.

Steady → Leadership
Programme management
Task Force training workshop and project launch
Project planning
Using standards
Producing the design proposal
Planning implementation
Task Force communication

Task Force training and project launch will follow on from executive workshops. A training workshop provides the best vehicle for combining training and project planning. There is information about Planning a Workshop in Section 3 Reference Material along with an illustration of a Task Force programme and many of the tools and techniques which the team will need.

This is an overview of the overall process and typical timings:

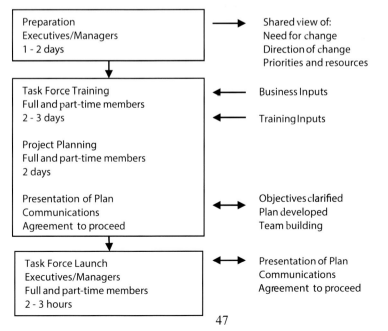

47

This is an Input/Output diagram for a Task Force training workshop:

Inputs	Task Force Training Workshop	Outputs
Business Strategy		Shared Vision
Benchmark information		Task Force –
Organisation Operation	Education	agreed role and
Training	Training	structure
Change Methodology	Team building	Working as a team
Draft project scope	Project planning	Agreed Project Scope
and objectives		Objectives and Project Plan
Facilitator	Presentation prepared	Communications Plan
Workshop Program		

The duration is likely to be between 4 and 5 days and should be held off site away from the day-to-day pressures of the organisation that might otherwise distract Task Force members. If possible, it should also be residential. The training is an opportunity to create a team that bonds together and believes it can deliver the objectives. An experienced facilitator should be used to oversee the programme.

The content needs to be suitable for all staff, whatever their past training or experience. Some of the team members may fear that they will not be able to cope with the training material. Many of them will not have made a presentation or even spoken out in public. All the tools and techniques that are illustrated in Section 3 Reference Material are easy to learn and can be practiced during the session. The use of techniques like "brainstorming" and the use of white boards and flip charts will give practice in presentation skills right from the outset.

Business inputs should include briefings about the organisation, its performance and how it works. These should be provided by the Sponsor and other leadership colleagues. This not only imparts knowledge, it is an opportunity for the Leadership Team to demonstrate commitment and (if they stay for lunch or dinner) for staff to meet the Task Force in an informal setting.

Other inputs include:

- Why the project is being undertaken.
- The working of the areas of the business being changed.
- The methodology that is being proposed with all the necessary tools and techniques.
- How to manage the people aspects of change.
- The project scope and objectives.
- Project management guidance.

An essential part of the training for a Task Force is to introduce the Transition Curve – see Section 3 Reference Material for an explanation. This helps the team to anticipate the reactions of others to change and also to begin planning a response. Force Field Analysis can be used to develop discussion about the change management specifics of the organisation and to plan how the Task Force might handle the opportunities for involvement and communication.

There is little to be gained by imposing project objectives that the Task Force feel are unrealistic. Time needs to be set aside during the training programme for the team to review the proposed project scope and objectives and to discuss them with the Sponsor. In addition, any significant issues that arise during the workshop need to be clarified and resolved.

The Task Force then need to prepare a first pass project plan, a briefing presentation for the Steering Group and, if necessary, a presentation to the Leadership Team. When agreed by the Steering Group, all this material becomes the basis for the project launch and first Task Force communication.

A formal high profile launch of the project by Task Force members often follows on directly from the workshop and executive approval. Attendance at the launch will vary but often includes managers, supervisors and staff representatives. It is often held on the last afternoon of the workshop and is an opportunity to:

- Raise the profile of Task Force members

- Communicate the need for change and the plans that have been developed

- Reinforce the commitment of the Leadership Team to the change process.

Finally the Task Force needs to review and confirm the facilities they will use when back on site. Typically:

- a dedicated office near the centre of the target improvement area

- basic office equipment including PCs and network access

- flip charts and white boards

In the spirit of "no secrets - no surprises" the area should be readily accessible to all staff.

Steady → Leadership
        Programme management
        Task Force training workshop and project launch
        Project planning
        Using standards
        Producing the design proposal
        Planning implementation
        Task Force communication

First pass project plans will have been prepared during the Task Force training workshop and will be developed and refined during the Steady phase. The best advice to the Task Force is to 'keep it simple'.

The Task Force should follow these steps to plan the project:

• Read the Project Brief to ensure everyone understands and accepts the challenge. Ensure that any anomalies or differences are thoroughly discussed and resolved.

• Produce an Input/Output diagram for the project. The outputs will demonstrate that the Task Force understands their objectives.

• Prepare a networked input-output diagram which clarifies the project stages. This will ensure that the Task Force understands the sequence of data collection, analysis and at what stage the overall deliverables of the project need to be completed.

• Decide on the timescales for each stage. The Task Force should take a forward looking view (i.e. how long they think each stage should take) and backwards view (i.e. planning the project completion in a tight but feasible time). It is important that the team distinguish between actions which are largely in their control and those where they are dependent on others to provide information or views e.g. during data collection.

• Produce a plan for the project. As a rule of thumb; for the design stages of a project which are largely in the control of the team and which take 4 weeks or more, the plan can show tasks by week. The Task Force should highlight important dependencies particularly for external support.

• Prepare communications information including alterations / acceptance of the Project Brief, the project plan and feedback / acceptance of the project management structure.

An individual project plan will contain some standard elements:

- Communications.
- Data Collection.
- Analysis.
- Option development and selection.
- Proposal formulation.
- Benefit analysis.
- Risk analysis.

Project planning software and sophisticated process analysis and process mapping tools are available. These may look impressive and in the right hands they may work well but, almost by definition, their use will concentrate the analysis in the hands of the specialists and reduce the level of team ownership.

A high level plan with several teams might look like this:

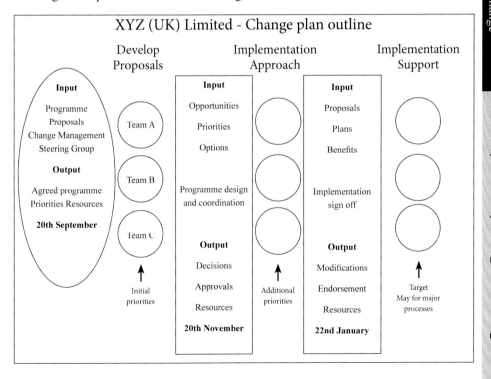

This simplified high level plan has a number of benefits:

- It is part of the "buy in" process for the Leadership Team.

- It summarises the teams which are being launched and the review and target dates which have been agreed.

- It is a useful programme summary for communication throughout the organisation

- It introduces the concept of Input - Output analysis.

One client adopted a programme review process using "approval gates" to control the design and implementation process:

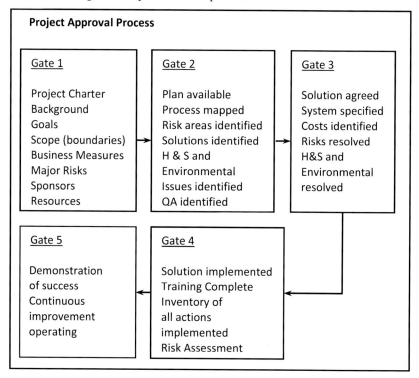

Project Approval Process

Gate 1	Gate 2	Gate 3
Project Charter Background Goals Scope (boundaries) Business Measures Major Risks Sponsors Resources	Plan available Process mapped Risk areas identified Solutions identified H & S and Environmental Issues identified QA identified	Solution agreed System specified Costs identified Risks resolved H&S and Environmental resolved

Gate 5	Gate 4	
Demonstration of success Continuous improvement operating	Solution implemented Training Complete Inventory of all actions implemented Risk Assessment	

The client established a steering group which monitored the progress of all major change initiatives. The Task Force Leader presented progress at a weekly review. Projects were not allowed to proceed to the next stage until the success criteria for each gate were achieved and signed off. This gate process provides a structure for the project plan for each Task Force. It is also an example of using standards.

Steady → Leadership
       Programme management
       Task Force training workshop and project launch
       Project planning
       Using standards
       Producing the design proposal
       Planning implementation
       Task Force communication

The use of standards ensures that Task Forces adopt a consistent style and avoids duplication of effort. Often standards are developed by the first Task Force and then incorporated into the training for subsequent teams.

Examples of using standards:

• Document standards e.g. templates, naming, version control, storage facilities.

• Common measures of performance and how these are measured, displayed and actioned.

• A common approach to training across all teams. Note it is essential that all teams have all the capabilities they require, including to provide on-the-job training within the team.

• The best ways of managing teams e.g. use of meetings, measures, briefings and team-building events.

• Common job role descriptions e.g. for team leaders, operators, developers, support staff. This will ensure flexibility, mobility and professional development.

• Layout standards e.g. furniture, decoration, offices vs. open plan, signage.

Standards should reflect both an agreed common practice in the organisation and best practice in the industry.

Steady - Using standards

Steady → Leadership
        Programme management
        Task Force training workshop and project launch
        Project planning
        Using standards
        Producing the design proposal
        Planning implementation
        Task Force communication

The Task Force must follow an agreed methodology. This should be identified when the Project Brief is developed and explained to the Task Force (with the optional use of a case study) during the training. This methodology should form the foundation of the approach and plan that the Task Force describe at the Launch.

There are two main types of improvement methodologies:

> • Organisation design methodology e.g. business process redesign.

> • Problem solving methodology e.g. aspects of Kaizen and quality improvement tools.

Organisation redesign projects will use a design methodology but problem solving methodology is often used to address particular issues e.g. a specific product quality problem. Problem solving methods are also invaluable after the implementation of design proposals and should form part of implementation training.

Much organisation design methodology is based on the ideas of Michael Porter, Michael Hammer & James Champy and John Parnaby. The philosophy is straightforward:

> • Organisations exist to serve customers and for the benefit of stakeholders.

> • They have primary processes which provide that service and secondary processes which keep the organisation working.

> • People and technology are employed to ensure the processes operate effectively.

> • Measures of success vary but would often include: market share, profitability and customer service.

A redesign of the organisation looks deceptively simple:

> a) Identify the main processes in the organisation and prepare a process model.

> b) Benchmark and collect customer feedback for each major process.

54

c) Map the existing processes.

d) Generate a concept design. Often there are a number of options that will need to be evaluated.

e) Establish priorities for detailed design.

f) Detailed design.

g) Implementation.

Further information about benchmarking, customer feedback and developing a concept design is included in Section 3 - Reference Material.

Quick Wins

Task Forces often uncover opportunities for change which can be readily implemented and provide tangible, rapid benefits to the organisation. These are called quick wins, quick hits or golden nuggets. It is important that quick wins do not become a distraction from the project objectives, but provide extra benefit and credibility for the Task Force. Where possible the team should pass the responsibility for the implementation of these changes to line managers.

Steady → Leadership
                Programme management
                Task Force training workshop and project launch
                Project planning
                Using standards
                Producing the design proposal
                Planning implementation
                Task Force communication

Implementation should be planned in phases. This will ensure that changes are working effectively and that enough Task Force support is available at each stage. The first phase of implementation is often called a demonstrator, because it "demonstrates" the effectiveness of the principles that underpin the transformation and the benefits that will be delivered. In addition, a demonstrator allows lessons to be learned to guide future implementations.

Implementation is focussed on a selected team or process i.e. to deliver as many aspects of the change as possible in one area. The alternative of implementing a narrow aspect of the proposals on a broad front (e.g. training, physical reorganisation) will add to the management complexity and will delay the delivery of benefits and success.

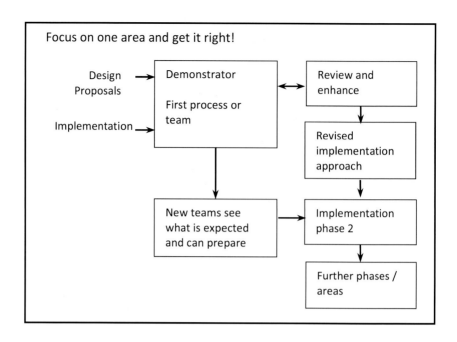

Focussing by team or process will yield early visible benefits and will allow the Task Force to learn implementation lessons that can be carried forward to future implementations.

If the first area is to be a "demonstrator" of good practice, the Task Force needs to work with the staff in that area to get the implementation right. Some organisations use implementation audits as part of the approval process. It is vital that subsequent teams on the implementation path are able to see what is expected and are able to prepare themselves for their turn.

A transformation project is only complete when new ways of working are fully embedded in the hearts, hands and minds of those who add value in the organisation. The project plan needs to include the deployment of the Task Force during implementation:

• Retain the core of the team to ensure understanding of the design proposals and continuity in successful approaches e.g. involvement and communication.

• Add in specialist skills to help with specific implementation issues e.g. IT expertise, office / factory layout, engineering, HR. These people are likely to be part-time throughout the project or full-time for a short burst of work.

- Ensure that those who will take operational responsibility are members of the Task Force. Bring them in to the team if they are not already members.

- Start the Change stage with another period of Task Force training and planning, and another launch event focussing on the approaches required for implementation. Retain the disciplines around managing the Task Force e.g. meetings and reviews.

During the design activities of the Steady stage, the activities largely lie inside the control of the Task Force and some flexibility is possible. During implementation, the Task Force will rely on non-team members e.g. external suppliers for the delivery of equipment, internal specialists with other responsibilities and the change will impact the operation of the organisation. Project planning needs to be of a high standard:

- Plan forwards by planning dependent tasks sequentially.

- Plan backwards by starting with a clear description of all that needs to be in place to deliver the end goal and then plan how each element is put in place. Use physical mock-ups, role playing, simulations, drawings, input-output diagrams etc. to describe the end goal ensuring the involvement of those who will run the area.

Finally, plan to realise the benefits and make them visible. Some implementation projects focus on the physical deliverables but fall short of the actions required to realise all the benefits.

Steady → Leadership
        Programme management
        Task Force training workshop and project launch
        Project planning
        Using standards
        Producing the design proposal
        Planning implementation
        Task Force communication

The Communication Plan should be agreed at the Project Launch and its effectiveness reviewed at meetings with the Sponsor. The Plan will describe what the Task Force will do to keep the project stakeholders (including the staff of the organisation) informed of progress. It should also describe the management support they might need to do this, remembering that some proposals may be contentious.

The plan should cover the following elements:

- Weekly updates to all stakeholders e.g. newsletters (paper or email), presentations.

- Project Reviews.

- Organisation-wide communication post-review presentations, particularly at decision points.

- Workshops to promote the involvement of both senior and junior stakeholders e.g. review of data collection and analysis; evaluation of design options. For staff this may take the form of a "Tool Box" meeting – a briefing using a flip chart at the place of work.

- Communication of major deliverables e.g. presentations, route shows.

- Identify which member of the Task Force will take the co-ordination role for Project Communications.

The Task Force also need to agree their internal communication. Good practice includes:

- Daily-start up meetings for all full-time Task Force members - to focus the team on the tasks for the day. Time should be allocated to discuss particular issues that need resolution.

- Weekly planning meetings for all Task Force members - to focus on the overall plan and what needs starting, finishing or planning in the next week.

- Informal weekly review with Sponsor - to ensure that the Sponsor is familiar with the latest progress, the content of key deliverables and has given support to resolving critical issues.

- Daily Log recording all informal issues, required actions or significant events not recorded elsewhere.

- Standards covering templates (for presentations and documents) and document naming conventions, document storage and retrieval etc.

- Specific team responsibilities agreed in addition to the role of the Task Force Leader e.g. configuration manager for project documentation, communication manager.

The Task Force in one client used this graphic to illustrate that it was at the hub of communications relating to the change programme:

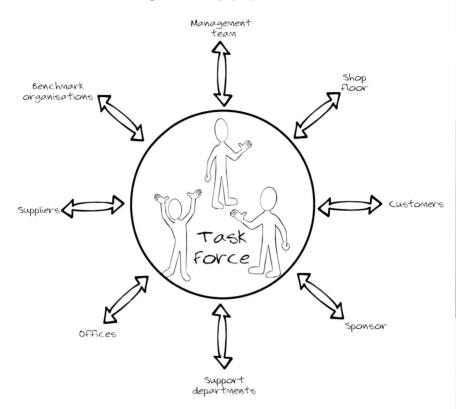

Check

The Sponsor and the Task Force Leader need to check that all is well before proceeding.

Prepare an audit checklist. Some organisations run a quality audit on implementation plans before they are signed off. Others have prepared an "implementation audit" process. It may take an extra few days but is well worth the effort.

Congratulations
you are ready to
implement!

Change

This phase includes the implementation of agreed proposals for change and the initiation of ongoing improvement processes.

As expressed in the following Input / Output diagram, this phase includes the implementation of the design proposals and the achievement of the agreed objectives i.e. the delivery of the benefit on which the change was predicated:

Inputs	Change	Outputs
Task force		Design proposals
Implementation plan		implemented
Executive leadership	**New process implementation**	Objectives met
Executive support		Trained staff
Objectives	**Staff selection & Training**	Improvement process in place
Change methodology		
Agreed design	**Project Handover**	Check lists complete
Procedures		Communications
Training material		Project sign off
Staff selection	**Delivering the benefit**	Feed-forward to next
Training sessions		project
Check lists	**On-going improvement**	Celebrate success
Communications		
	Communications	

Work involved in the implementation phase can vary enormously from project to project. It will involve detailed work as the benefits of a transformation project can only be achieved when the new ways of working are embedded in the heads, hearts and hands of those who add value in the organisation. In order to describe the key implementation issues, the guide assumes that implementation of the transformation proposals includes new methods of working based in teams, staff selection and training and the handover to operational management.

Change → **Leadership**
New process implementation
Selecting and training staff
Project Handover
Delivering the benefit
Ongoing improvement
Communications and visibility

Change - Leadership

At the point of implementation, leadership remains critical. It is vital for leaders to grasp this as often their interest has moved on to other initiatives before the project has arrived at the Change Phase leaving the project vulnerable at the most important stage i.e. when the implementation steps are due to deliver the intended benefit.

The transition curve, which we considered earlier, can be used to identify the specific challenges of this stage.

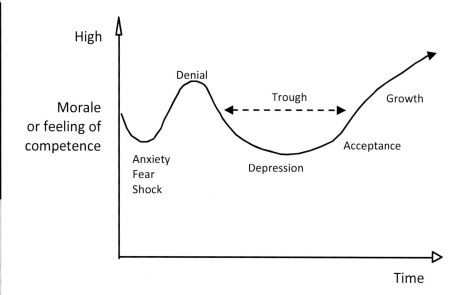

We discussed earlier the responsibilities of the wider leadership team (the Sponsor, Task Force Leader and operational managers) for creating an environment in which people feel challenged, but not threatened. We also described the importance of raising awareness of the need for change, establishing a vision, creating involvement and providing education and training, all underpinned by a committed programme of open communication.

This early work will have moved people through the valley of fear and passed the false dawn of denial but it is only in the change phase, as work is implemented, that staff will move through depression to acceptance and growth. The critical elements of effective leadership in this phase are:

> • Creating involvement around deciding on the final details of how major operations are to be completed and how work and the workplace are organised.

- Delivering on-the-job training that builds fluency and confidence (rather than tell and run).

- Providing further education that helps individuals to buy in to the principles that underpin the transformation.

- Developing a team ethos during workshops and training sessions that creates supportive relationships.

- Ensuring access to managers and their open engagement with the staff in the Change phase.

- Sustaining the open communication delivered in earlier stages.

The Sponsor should oversee the style of the implementation whilst relying on others to deliver specific actions:

- Leadership team and Senior Management colleagues.

- The Task Force Leader.

- The line managers and team leaders of the parts of the organisation where change is imminent.

- Staff directly involved in the change, for example Task Force members and critical technical staff.

All of these people are vital to the success of the transformation and they will all appear excited by the ideas and prospects, however they too will be going through the transition curve and will have concerns and fears about what is to come:

- The Sponsor will have fears arising from the uncertainty of success and from the loss of control as a result of a focus on involvement.

- The Task Force Leader will feel apprehensive about the chances of success, what the future will hold and their competence to deliver.

- Task Force members will have fears about what comes next for them and about the responses of their peer group to their close involvement in transformation.

- Managers and team leaders who will be responsible for the redesigned organisation will be concerned about their competence to deliver and whether they will receive the support they need especially if performance comes under executive scrutiny.

Despite all our efforts some staff will remain concerned, others will be in denial and others hostile. The leadership team need to remain committed to the good practice of the approach.

The approach of MBWA (managing by walking about) continues to be one of the best ways of sensing the morale of the organisation. In particular practical examples of peoples' concerns are worth seeking out.

> For example: A Task Force was planning the redesign of a large component machining facility in an aerospace factory. The plant layout, material flow, material control systems, team organisation, roles and responsibilities and payment systems were all being changed. The Task Force had delivered extensive training, the trade unions were on board and most of the staff seemed happy with the prospect. However the Task Force Leader noticed that two of the team seemed antagonistic. Ten minutes discussion revealed that they had worked in the factory for 20 years and had always worked on adjacent machines. They didn't want to be separated.

It may not have been possible to address their particular concern, but this example highlights the need to see the change from the other person's perspective. The Task Force Leader was practising NEMAWASHI (see Section 3 Reference Material), though he didn't know it at the time.

How decisions are made will be another area that will become a point of tension during the change phase, because it will be important to balance timeliness (ie effective decision-making to maintain momentum) and the involvement of staff in these decisions. One temptation might be to refer every decision to wider involvement, slowing the project down, whilst on the other hand, fluent decision-making by the Task Force Leader or Sponsor might remove the opportunity for a wider decision process. The one area that can often appear a straightforward one for decisions is appointments of people to particular roles. These are rarely standalone decisions as they impact other roles and it may be better to have more open selection process rather than using direct appointments.

It is strongly recommended that an implementation steering group is created to manage the progress of the implementation and to oversee the critical decisions. It is recommended that this group is chaired by the Sponsor, meets weekly and includes the Task Force Leader, critical members of Task Force, the managers in the new management structure and critical support staff (eg HR, Finance, Engineering, IT).

Change → Leadership
New process implementation
Selecting and training staff
Project Handover
Delivering the benefit
Ongoing improvement
Communications and visibility

Change - New process implementation

The implementation of a new (transformed) process will require the development of many detailed aspects of the working operations. The work in the Steady Phase will provide much design detail but this will need further detailing during implementation.

Inputs	Team and process	Outputs
→		→
Materials / Information	- workplace - method - equipment - consumables - tools - management	Products / Services plus Measurements

These specific elements include:

• The product or service to be delivered, including how the quality will be assured and how it will be delivered to the customer.

• The direct materials or information from which the product will be created, including how it is received by the team.

• The sequence of operations by which the product or service will be created, the method describing these operations and the ways in which the team members will know that what they have created will meet the necessary specification.

• The people capabilities required to completed these operations, the job roles needed and therefore the type of people appropriate for the team.

• The equipment, tools (including IT systems and infrastructure) and consummables needed and how these will be obtained, maintained and calibrated.

• The workplace layout for the area in which the work will be undertaken including features to facilitate good team functioning.

• The team management methods required to bring together all these elements to produce the product /service and to ensure that this happens consistently over time, including measures of performance.

The best way to develop this detail will be to use workshops with the chosen team, supported by technical staff (eg quality, engineering, IT) for deciding and describing what needs to be done. The starting point will be the design work

Change - New process implementation

of the Steady Phase. It is strongly recommended that the team trial all proposed approaches (both in workshops or the live environment) and that complex solutions to problems are only added once the basic operations are running in pilot – start simple.

It will be critical for the team to look at the logistical and maintenance support of all these elements eg how materials will get to the point of use, how equipment and tooling will be calibrated and maintained, and how team members will be selected and trained both at the start and on an ongoing basis.

One particular area worthy of comment is the method for describing the operations. It is vital that the team agree a method by which they will complete each specific operation in order to delivery a fault-free and timely output. This method will then form the basis for training and improvement (ie if someone thinks of a better way to complete the operations the team should trial it and amend the method with any agreed change).

Change → Leadership
New process implementation
Selecting and training staff
Project Handover
Delivering the benefit
Ongoing improvement
Communications and visibility

A change programme often results in a radical redesign and it is likely that the number of staff required, their job grades, skill requirements and flexibility will all change.

The organisation will need a consistent policy to address the appointment of staff to the redesigned structure. This can be through a top down appointment process or through advertising posts and seeking applicants, depending on staff agreements, current practice and national employment legislation. Advertising posts and seeking applicants usually gives good and felt-fair results.

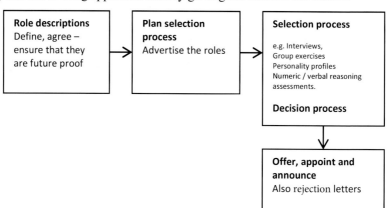

Training, involvement and communications are at the core of the Change stage. Promote involvement through using workshops to develop areas of detail for implementation, for example:

- Finalising office / shop floor layout.
- Developing the detailed operational procedures.
- Trialling the screens for the new computer system.

Involvement may seem to take longer than telling, but people engage if they are contributing rather than sitting and listening. It will build commitment and the outcomes will be improved.

In the early project stages the focus was "Education": raising awareness of need for change and competitive practice.

In the later stages, detailed "how to" hands on training programmes and process trialling will become more commonplace.

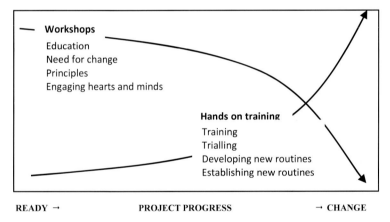

"Hands on" training sessions are time consuming to develop and deliver but it is vital that they are delivered well:

"Nearly good enough is not good enough!"

Allow sufficient time in the plan, particularly for the early training events.

Many organisations that introduce "team based" processes also use a team based training matrix, which is displayed, in the team area. These are sometimes called ILU or 5* training matrices. They make visible the team's progress in staff development and the extent of "coverage" within the team.

More information and a further example are included in Section 3 Reference Material – Team training 5*.

More information and a further example are included in Section 3 Reference Material – Team training 5*.

Change → Leadership
New process implementation
Selecting and training staff
Project Handover
Delivering the benefit
Ongoing improvement
Communications and visibility

Project handover is the most critical part of the change process as this is the point at which the Task Force pass the responsibility for operations to the operational management teams. An example of how this handover might be approached is as follows:

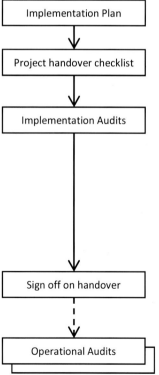

Monitor

Handover Criteria

Progress to the "Go-live" point should be monitored against established criteria on a regular basis (e.g. weekly) using a Red, Amber, Green (traffic light) status or a completeness score.

The scoring should be a mutual decision between the Task Force and the Operational Team and if the criteria are well set then the score and the reasons should be clear. As the go-live approaches, the reviews will become more frequent e.g. moving to daily.

The "Go-Live" decision should be formal

Operational audits should be used to check that the redesigned organisation is performing as expected and that ongoing improvements are being achieved. They may be a simplified version of the implementation audit.

For some organisations this list may seem an "overkill", for others standard business practice. An example of an implementation audit is included with Section 3 Reference Material.

The Sponsor and the Leadership team should ensure that success is celebrated and publicised and the project handover is an obvious point at which to do this. Celebrations provide the opportunity to reinforce the vision behind the transformation, recognise the hard work of the Task Force and to encourage the Operational Team as they take the work forward. Choose a style of celebration that can be repeated across the organisation as nothing can engender a feeling of unfairness more than to see early successes celebrated with great flourish but later successes barely noticed.

Change → Leadership
New process implementation
Selecting and training staff
Project Handover
Delivering the benefit
Ongoing improvement
Communications and visibility

Transformation projects will, almost without exception, require a significant expenditure and a business case will need to be generated to justify the work. The anticipated financial benefits of the project will have been laid out in the business case and these will generally be either through a reduction in costs or an increase in revenue. The project or programme should not be closed until these benefits have been delivered for the following reasons:

1. The benefits were part of the project proposal (contract).

2. Implementation actions may have been omitted and the failure to achieve the benefits will highlight this. For example, a manufacturing redesign led to a reduction in manufacturing lead-time but not to the reduction in work-in-progress inventories expected because the lead-times were not updated in the planning system. By tracking the inventory reduction (or the lack of it) this anomaly was detected and corrected.

3. Lessons about delivering benefits need to be learned for future projects.

4. Benefits make good PR and help spur further work.

In order for the benefits to be tracked it is important to measure the benefit itself and to track the milestones relating to the delivery of the benefit (e.g. the implementation of measures) and indicators of the implementation steps (e.g.

number of sales visits). These measures are illustrated in the following table:

Benefit type	Benefit measure e.g.	Milestones e.g.	Indicators e.g.
Revenue increase	Track revenue increase by customer segment	Implementation measure; development of publicity material; training for sales team.	Number of sales visits; number of quotes requested / delivered.
Cost reduction	Measure cost reduction by cost type e.g. materials, stock, labour.	Implementation measure; supplier conference held; manufacturing operations simplified; employee consultations started.	Cost savings delivered to budget.

These measures will almost certainly need to be implemented before go-live to provide a baseline against which to measure the effect of the change.

Change → Leadership
New process implementation
Selecting and training staff
Project Handover
Delivering the benefit
Ongoing improvement
Communications and visibility

World Class organisations only achieve and maintain that position by ensuring continuous improvement in their operations. Basic continuous improvement principles, tools and techniques should be included in implementation training for all staff and embedded in the management practices of the new team structures.

There are a number of methodologies, based on the work of W. Edwards Deming, that create a drive to ongoing improvement which World Class organisations have found particularly effective. We will describe the practical aspects of embedding these practices into the Change Phase of a transformation project, whilst more comprehensive explanations can be found elsewhere.

A continuous improvement approach can be initiated in the team meetings of the new organisation by identifying and implementing ideas that address problem areas. Often team members will think of improvement ideas but the lack of the appropriate tools will mean that they are not recognised and captured.

OFI (Opportunity for Improvement)

Idea	Plan	Do	Check	Act	Complete
Idea 4					Idea 1
		Idea3			
			Idea 2		

A simple OFI (Opportunity for Improvement) Board is a straightforward first step. This works well for quick wins (i.e. where the problem investigation can be straight forward and the implementation simple). The OFI board will demonstrate how many ideas are being generated as well as encouraging implementation.

Notes

- Ideas are written on Post It notes. Add the date to track progress.

- All ideas offered are listed on the board and then owned by the team.

- Ideas follow the PDCA cycle (the Deming Cycle) and are moved on as agreed.

- More complex ideas should be allocated to a Directed Improvement Group.

- Continuous improvement should be on the agenda for the team meeting and at that point ideas added and monitored.

A Directed Improvement Group is a part-time team that operates in the style of a conventional project team. The group is established to address a specific and significant problem affecting the work team and the group is staffed by people chosen to address the particular issue. The group members should be trained in a continuous improvement methodology and the associated techniques. It would also be sensible to provide training to address the particular problem e.g. quality improvement, set up time reduction, process improvement.

A Continuous Improvement Group is usually based around the work team and with occasional support from specialists. The group themselves and not the team leader or manager choose the issues to be addressed. Following a well-implemented change, the issues that need addressing will be apparent to the whole working team based on their own experience and the visible measures of performance. The team members voluntarily participate in improvement – it is something they want to do because they want the team to improve. The group

Change - Ongoing improvement

can plan time to work on improvement ideas during the working day provided they meet their agreed output targets.

Improvement is part of everyone's role and part of the normal way of working. Paying for improvement is best avoided as payment often requires independent evaluation and this stifles ownership and innovation. Recognition of good and well implemented ideas however should be encouraged.

Change → Leadership
New process implementation
Selecting and training staff
Project Handover
Delivering the benefit
Ongoing improvement
Communications and visibility

Communications relating to the ongoing operation of the new process is vital. This is separate and distinct from project communication. A communication structure should be implemented during the change phase, with the key players being trained in effective communication methods. This will include the agreed routine and predictable processes. Section 3 Reference Material contains extra detail and there is a wealth of information available online.

Key features of an effective communications structure are:

- Daily team meetings with a standard agenda

- Weekly/Monthly business updates

- Newsletters e.g. monthly

- Annual events often including family members

The core meeting for the team is "The Daily Stand-up Meeting". It is remarkable that many organisations feel that a daily meeting is "over-kill" or a waste of time.

The features which make a Stand-up Meeting effective are:

- Predictable and standard approach for the organisation - same time every day, timed at the beginning of the working day (or shift). Some organisations record attendance - latecomers stand out!

- All team members attend unless they are away.

- Fixed duration: 10 minutes

- Standard agenda: e.g.

    Review yesterday's results (measures of performance)

    Issues that may impact today's achievement

    Improvement actions

    Organisation news e.g. visitors.

The Task Force should continue to provide regular communication updates throughout the Change period - typically through special meetings, newsletters and road shows, as well as through the organisation's usual communication methods.

Visible Team Operations

Many organisations now encourage a very visible operating style and the team is often the building block of the structure. Teams benefit from an identifiable team area. Some common features are illustrated below.

Features often include:

> • A visible gateway for the control of materials coming in to the team area and product leaving with the team designation.

> • Visible work and maintenance schedules.

> • Visible measures of performance showing up to date results maintained by the team or team leader.

> • A visible training matrix.

> • Flip chart or white board for noting work problems and communication messages.

> • Continuous improvement area for showing analysis, actions, results and achievements.

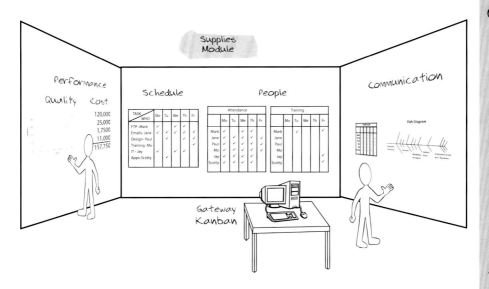

The goal is to create an area where the role and performance of the team is self-explanatory. The work area should encourage self-directed, flexible and team-based working. A new employee, customer or supplier should be able to understand the role of the team and its current performance without asking questions. The information on display should be self-explanatory.

Project Sign-off

Implementation is now complete. A formal project sign-off process, similar to the one used just prior to implementation, should be used to ensure that the Sponsor, Task Force Leader and the operational managers agree that the work of the Task Force has been completed. It is vital to note any lessons learned.

Regular audits and reviews of measures of performance should be used to establish that the changes are working as planned and that performance continues to improve as the experience of the team grows.

Feed-forward to next project

The Task Force and the operational team will need to work together to learn lessons from the change process. These along with the lessons that were noted at project sign-off, can be embedded in the training for future roll-out or transformational projects and act as a template for working check-lists or standard working practices. A programme or project lessons learned log may be a useful way of capturing lessons as they are learned.

At the end of the project Task Force members may be involved in further roll-out activities, return to their original roles or be redeployed in the changed organisation. Because the Ready Steady Change process is very developmental, it is usual for members of the Task Force to find that this experience acts as a spur to their future career opportunities.

Check

Post implementation audits can help ensure the new process and organisation are operating as planned. The information from audits can form one of the team measures of performance.

Section 3

Reference Material

This section of the guide addresses topics that are relevant throughout the Ready Steady Change process.

Customer feedback
Benchmarking the organisation
Planning a workshop
Example workshop programme
Developing a concept design
Looking for roadblocks

> Force field analysis
> Key relationship mapping
> Nemawashi

Communication for the change process
Analysis techniques

> Brainstorming
> SWOT analysis
> Input / output analysis
> Process modelling
> Process mapping
> Flowcharting
> Value analysis and value stream mapping
> Pareto analysis
> Classification by RRS - runners, repeaters and strangers
> Cause and effect analysis
> 5 Whys
> Risk analysis and FMEA

5 Ss for workplace organisation
Team measures of performance
Team training 5*
The transition curve
Implementation audit

Customer Feedback

Obtaining feedback from customers can help an organisation to understand the need for change and provide an insight into priorities and target levels of performance. Customers will usually be prepared to provide competitor comparisons and insights into competitor's performance and future plans.

There are three main classes of customer and all can provide useful feedback but the data should be analysed and maintained separately:

> • Lost customers: customers who have received goods or services in the past but who, for whatever reason, no longer do so.

> • Current customers: sometimes these are subdivided by significance (e.g. top 10) or geography or by type of service received. The best advice on classification is to "keep it simple".

> • Potential customers: e.g. we have quoted for their business but lost out to competitors; or target customers who have been identified but not yet quoted.

The next step is to identify "order-winning" and "order-qualifying" criteria. For example "price", "time to supply" and "product life" may be an order-winning criteria. "Reliability of the product" or "product performance" may be order qualifying. If we fail to satisfy order-qualifying criteria there is little chance of even being considered as a supplier. However, given that they will be achieved, further enhancing order qualifying performance will not necessarily enhance our prospects of winning the business. Any redesign of the organisation must result in qualifying criteria being met.

Which order winning criteria are most significant to the client? Most clients will say that price is critical, but often there are "trade-offs". For example, if the product life were to double would the client pay an extra 25%, or 35% or 50%? If the time to supply were reduced from 8 weeks to 2 weeks would the client pay more?

Trade off analysis provides a way to tackle these questions systematically. In the example below the client or prospective client is asked to complete the matrix by indicating their preference for each option using the numbers from 1 to 9, using each number only once. The trade-off in this case is between a change in product life and the product price, but any order winning criteria could have been selected. The range of choice offered needs to be realistic. Matrix box choices "1" and "9" are obvious and can be filled in beforehand. Any client will opt first for increased product life at a reduced cost, and increased price for reduced life will always be the least favourite option.

The interest comes in how the client completes the remaining squares in the matrix.

Trade off analysis

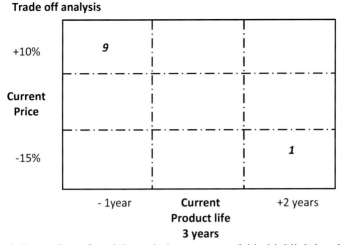

+10%

Current
Price

-15%

- 1year   **Current**   +2 years
Product life
3 years

Task Forces have found the technique very useful in highlighting the real requirements of customers. If they can meet these requirements through the redesign the business can be transformed.

The final step is to ask the client to rate the organisation's current performance on each of these criteria. Most clients will also be prepared to rate the performance of competitors. The results are shown graphically below. The most significant order-winning criteria is Criteria 1, then Criteria 2 etc.

In this example the analysis should cause concern. Whilst "our organisation" outperforms competitor 2, competitor 1 performs best in all the criteria that are

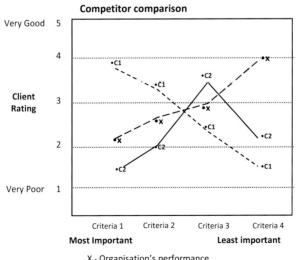

Competitor comparison

Very Good   5

4

Client
Rating   3

2

Very Poor   1

Criteria 1   Criteria 2   Criteria 3   Criteria 4
Most Important   **Least important**

X - Organisation's performance
C1- Competitor 1 performance
C2- Competitor 2 performance

77

most important to the client. How is competitor 1 achieving this level of performance?

In a transformational or process redesign project, this analysis should be used to set objective design criteria.

Benchmarking the organisation

Benchmarking should be a strategic issue for any organisation. Like customer feedback, it is a critical source of information about opportunities to improve. It is often the inspiration for executives to see the need for change and the direction and nature of the change. It is also the basis for establishing targets for change and involving staff in the organisation's vision. As we will see, information can come from enterprises that are unlike our own, we just need to know how to look and ask questions.

When changing spots it is important to understand not only target levels of performance but also the good practice that underpins superior performance. Benchmarking must include direct competition as well as other organisations working in a similar way in the same sector, regardless of territory. Take the advice of customers when choosing benchmark companies.

Levels and types of benchmarking are illustrated below using a private enterprise model, but the principles apply for any organisation:

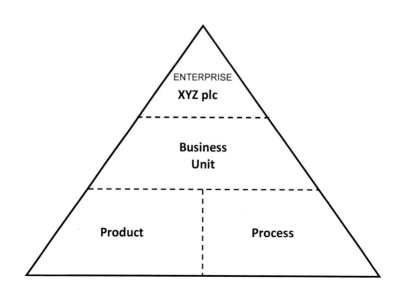

Enterprise benchmarking

The main question asked is how does the organisation compare with other enterprises (e.g. turnover, growth, profitability)? The question is answered by making comparisons between organisations in the same sector (e.g. banking, utilities, manufacturing, public sector, etc.). Global information is often readily available through published accounts, however large enterprises will include a number of businesses and the data will not be available at business unit level. That said, good practice may be read across from one sector to another (e.g. lean processes, quality, problems solving methods) and trends in enterprise level performance will be of interest, even though it may not be possible to determine the causes of a change in performance. In the case of public sector organisations, detailed comparisons and league tables are frequently in place. Library and internet searches may locate sector level reports that allow sector trends and comparisons between organisations to be made.

Business unit benchmarking

Real competition often occurs between organisations at this level and published data is usually much more difficult to find. There are organisations like PIMS Associates Inc ("The Profit Impact of Market Strategy (PIMS) database") that provide a specialist service with clients prepared to share data. Successful comparisons will normally require some more innovative approaches. For example, using customers, suppliers, academics or past employees to provide feedback on their knowledge of a competitor, getting to know competitors through trade bodies, or by attending conferences and exhibitions etc.

Some of your staff may interact with your competitors on a regular basis e.g.

- When bidding.

- When competitors are also customers or suppliers.

- When working on joint ventures or licencing arrangements.

- In the maintenance and support environment where they may see competitor products in service or the competitor's staff servicing products in the field.

Staff need to be made aware of the information the organisation requires.

International comparisons are vital but will need careful preparation and analysis. It is not uncommon for competitors to allow visits on a "quid pro quo" basis.

In the public sector international comparisons can be very illuminating though, of course, underlying values, demographics, etc. should be investigated to aid proper interpretation.

Product or service benchmarking

This is commonly practised by all product design and manufacturing units across the world. These exercises, especially when the physical product is obtained, provide invaluable insight into product features, patent protection issues and manufacturing costs and reliability. This approach can be read across to service organisations, for example the financial services sector that has increasingly treated it's offerings as a tangible product.

Process benchmarking

This is aimed at establishing a best in class view for each major core process. Core processes will depend on the organisation but example processes might include:

> Market awareness.
> Product innovation.
> Operations.
> Inbound Logistics.
> Sales.
> Market development.
> Distribution.

Organisations identify their key processes during transformation programmes and the benchmarking assists this work by showing the good practice that must be embedded into the transformed organisation. Process models have been developed for many types of enterprises through the work of Parnaby, Porter etc. For process benchmarking, the organisation being looked at will probably not be a competitor and therefore a free exchange of information (sometimes covered by confidentiality agreements) is possible. Visits to other organisations should be well documented e.g. in visit reports, good practice guides etc.

Unfortunately, there are still executives who rehearse their reasons for not doing benchmarking. Usually their organisations are in the "incumbents and monopolies" or sitting duck quadrant and for them complacency is a way of life - they have already 'done' benchmarking and are at the leading edge (ok, let's relax and go for a drink). Those less complacent would like to 'do benchmarking' but unfortunately, there are no equivalent organisations in the world. This demonstrates a lack of drive, imagination and understanding.

In world-class organisations process ownership is clear and process improvement are a day-to-day activity. For them process benchmarking is a way of life.

"For us, the essence of effective leadership is precisely the art of mobilizing and pulling together the intellectual resources of all employees in the service of the firm. Only by drawing on the combined brainpower of all its employees can we succeed."

Konosuke Matsushita, Executive Director Matsushita Electric Industrial Company

In conclusion, benchmarking is important for establishing the art of the possible in terms of performance and working methods, and the Ready Steady Change approach provides an excellent vehicle for implementing the ideas from a benchmarking study. There are many reference works on benchmarking and these should be consulted for a more complete guide but the best experience will be gained by getting started.

Competition is like war! Get to know your enemy!

Planning a workshop

Reference is made to workshops throughout the Ready Steady Change process. The critical difference between a workshop and a training course is that there will be a tangible output that is agreed between those participating. Some of the basic good practice which applies to all workshops is covered in this section.

Preparation

- Write down the objectives of the workshop – make them as tangible as possible.

- Agree the attendees.

- Map out the decisions that are to be taken and the process to be followed based on the dependencies between them - produce a diagram.

- Decide what inputs will be required. This might include information about the organisation, training material, marketing material and how the decisions will be made e.g. in plenary or syndicates.

- Decide how the outputs will be shared and consolidated - all the team spirit will be lost if the attendees do not receive the outputs very soon after the workshop.

- Develop the agenda based on the decision process and a timescale based on the content. Workshops can take between 2 and 5 days.

- Test the proposal with a trusted colleague - one who understands the team. If this is new territory, seek advice from someone who is used to running such workshops.

- Agree the presenters and how facilitation will be handled.

• Choose and brief syndicate group leaders beforehand ensuring that they have been trained in the basic techniques.

• Discuss the event on a one-on-one basis with each of the attendees and presenters once the objectives and agenda are drafted but not frozen.

• Share the ideas behind the event with other managers and employee representatives. Reassure everyone that they will be briefed about outcomes.

• Agree the date and venue and communicate with attendees and presenters.

Location

• An off-site location will make it easier to keep attendees focussed on the task in hand and not distracted by the day job.

• Room - set up the tables in a U–shaped layout with the screen at the top end. Ensure that there is presentation equipment and sufficient flip charts. Arrange separate syndicate rooms with flip chats – participants may feel inhibited in their contributions if these can be overheard.

Attendees

• Keep the total number within a maximum of 15. Avoid part time attendees.

• Presenters - will depend on the objectives of the workshop, but consider inviting a customer to give their input on a key issue and perhaps invite them to attend a review at the end of the workshop. Make sure they are thanked after their presentation.

Distractions

•Mobiles and laptops must be managed. These should be switched off during sessions and preferably for the whole day.

Facilitation

• A good facilitator will assist the smooth flow of the workshop by promoting team work, ensuring that all voices are heard, that side-tracks are cut short and to provide an impartial challenge if issues are being sidestepped. Your instinct may be to use an internal facilitator or no facilitator at all, but beware the risk of reinforcing a "boss" culture.

Workshop breaks

- It is good to keep the team together for formal breaks like lunch. A working lunch can be effective.

- Regular (hourly) comfort breaks of 5 minutes work well in maintaining concentration levels but the duration needs to be agreed and kept.

Using syndicate groups

- These will enhance the number of people actively contributing, the quality of their contributions and will reduce the possibility of excessive groupthink. They will also allow different views to be taken or work to be completed in parallel.

- The make up of the groups and the syndicate questions should be developed beforehand. Group leaders should have been briefed and trained in brainstorming techniques.

- Ensure that groups are allowed to share their findings and that the full group reaches a conclusion.

Record the output

Review the objectives of the workshop and get the group to prepare their "findings, conclusions and / or action plan"

Communicate the output

Two main types of communication are common;

- A presentation to Executives with an opportunity for challenge/ questions.

- A written communication to other staff.

Follow-up

Follow up workshop(s) for other staff and employee representatives may be appropriate to ensure their engagement with the process and, wherever possible, these should follow the same style.

Actions

Ensure you personally monitor the completion of all actions.

Example workshop programme

This 5 day programme was designed for a Task Force who needed to prepare a plan to redesign the operations process in their organisation. None of the team had previous experience in change management or process redesign.

Task Force workshop - Operations Process Redesign Task Force

DAY 1

9.30am Reception and Coffee
Introduction and Personal introductions
Workshop objectives & Agenda
Business Need for Change
Developing Competitive Advantage through Process Redesign
Working Lunch
Re-Engineering the Organization
Analytical Techniques (Brainstorming, SWOT, Input/ Output analysis with examples and exercises) Process view of business
Team working principles
Task Force Project Brief
Syndicate Work - Business I/O analysis; Business process definition, Business process model; Feedback
Case Example of an organisation undertaking step change
5.00pm   Close

DAY 2

8.15am Review of Day 1
Business Inputs including update on Technical issues facing the organisation
Management of Change and Task Force Approach
Lunch
Syndicate Exercise - Implications of change at the site
Force field analysis; Feedback and discussion
6.00pm Close
Team dinner

DAY 3

8.15am   Review of Day 2
Control Systems Design Push v Pull
Levels of control Logistics in operation
Lunch
Communications Strategy
Review of Task Force Teams of Reference and Objectives
Project Planning
Review with Project Sponsor
5.00pm Close

DAY 4

8.15am Project planning
Review with Project Sponsor
5.00pm Close

DAY 5

8.15am Preparation for Project Launch
Review with Project Sponsor
Project Launch
Project Planning
Agree Communications plan
Close

The sequence of the input sessions and the initial syndicate exercises is important. These are educational and will give the Task Force confidence. There is no need to overplan the work in Days 4 and 5. The team have a lot to achieve at this stage, but it is a good idea for the Sponsor and the Facilitator to be available for consultation and advice during this time. This programme can be readily adapted for other types of Task Force.

Developing a concept design

A Concept Design describes the anticipated future shape of the organisation i.e. the outcome of the successful improvement programme. Like a blueprint, it shows the outline of what things will be like rather than the full detail. In large organisations, the Concept Design may be developed at company, division or business unit level, depending on the focus of change and the degree of managerial autonomy.

The Concept Design needs to be agreed by the Leadership Team as a basis for establishing priorities and the detailed design. It is often used to:

- Produce the initial business case for the improvement programme by enabling the costs and benefits to be estimated.

- Decide on the prioritised improvement projects / initiatives that will make up the programme so that project briefs can be developed.

- Brief those running the improvement projects, along with the vision, so that they can understand their role in the whole improvement programme.

- Monitor the deliverables from the improvement programme (the Concept Design should be a baseline document for the programme).

The Concept Design may need to be revised as the separate improvement projects deliver more detailed designs.

How detailed should the Concept Design be?

The Concept Design should provide the shape of the future organisation. It will show the major processes and the way that responsibility for the processes will be organised. It may include estimates of resources required to make the change as well as the impact on the organisation's performance when the change is fully implemented.

The Concept Design will be detailed enough to provide estimates of the costs, benefits and timescales, though excessive detail at this stage should be avoided because that will:

- Reduce the ownership of the Task Forces who will become responsible for the detailed design.

• Stifle innovation by making it more like a specification / design-led programme rather than a transformation led one.

• Delay the improvement projects which will in turn delay the delivery of the benefits.

Who should develop the Concept Design and how?

There are two main options:

1. Executive Team-led. This is appropriate if the executive team have the time and are prepared to develop the concept based on information collected rather than preconceived ideas. A combination of workshops and individual working can be used to deliver the Concept Design.

2. Task Force-led (see Steady section). The Task Force should be led and staffed by your own employees, though external support (for consultancy or facilitation) may be essential if the organisation has no experience of this way of working. The work of building the Need for Change and creating the Vision for Change could be added in to the scope of the Task Force, though in both cases the team is likely to provide inputs to the work of the Executive rather than replacing it.

Creating a Task Force to do this work will be very visible in your organisation and so it is best to communicate the Need for Change and Vision before the team is pulled together, in effect kicking off the whole area of communication and involvement.

A concept design in a simple manufacturing organisation might generate an output like the one below.

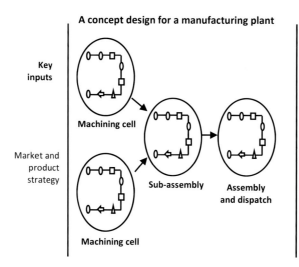

A concept design for a manufacturing plant

Key inputs

Machining cell

Market and product strategy

Machining cell

Sub-assembly

Assembly and dispatch

Key Outputs

Make v buy
Cellular v functional
Runners/Repeaters
Strangers
Shared resources
Choice of demonstrators for detail design and implementation

The schematic outlines the likely organisation and the output includes reference to the main strategic decisions.

Looking for roadblocks

The focus here will be the use of three related techniques that can help to avoid or minimise resistance to change:

- Force Field Analysis.
- Key Relationship Mapping.
- Nemawashi.

These techniques can also help identify under-used assets and opportunities to promote change.

Force field analysis

This technique can be used by leaders or teams to help identify potential issues. Resistance to change must be expected and Force field analysis can be used to anticipate the reasons and find ways to manage them.

Typically the steps are:

- Identify the stakeholders.
- Anticipate their issues.
- Estimate the size and impact of their concerns.
- Develop an action plan.

Potential stakeholders might include:

External	Internal
Shareholders	Executives
Clients	Directors /managers
Potential clients	Team leaders
Suppliers	Marketing staff
Agents	Other Staff
Other	Staff or union representatives

For a particular stakeholder, consider their issues and whether they will drive or resist the planned change. These issues may be personal or professional and may relate to the person themselves or others. An analysis pro-forma is provided below:

Force Field Analysis		
← Resisting -5 4 -3 -2 -1	Force Name	Driving → 1 2 3 4 5

This method is based on looking at change from the current position of the organisation. If the organisation is to move forward then forces will need to drive it on whilst, inevitably, some forces will resist this move. This method is used to think through actions that might be taken to enhance the driving forces and to reduce the impact of the resisting forces.

The analysis can be undertaken alone or as part of a workshop with your Leadership Team. It will also help flush out critical issues if it is included as part of a training programme with middle managers and employee representatives and as part of the Task Force training.

There are no right or wrong answers but every comment will reflect a real perception. Surprising, unusual or inconsistent comments are worth pursuing since they can provide a whole new perspective on the organisation.

Develop an action plan for the activities needed to encourage the driving forces or reduce the resisting forces and monitor the plan regularly. Some issues may naturally be picked up later in the programme (e.g. by the Task Force) and if so, there is no need to deal with things that could be left until later.

The following example is based on a plan developed by a steering group in advance of a change programme.

In this example, both the driving and resisting forces were identified and actions proposed. The estimate of the impact helped identify priority actions. Much of the benefit of the approach comes from giving systematic attention to the issues and a shared recognition of what is important.

Force Field Analysis - Driving Forces

Value Now	Force	Action	Expected Value
5	Customer demands	Improve communications of customer views	9
4	Leadership Team support	Use presentations to demonstrate commitment	6
6	Commitment of staff	Initiate training/ awareness programme	7
8	Task Force Approach	Ensure it is well supported	7
5	Clarity of message	Ensure the need for change and Vision are well presented	6

Force Field Analysis - Resisting Forces

9	Focus on Efficiency	Introduce customer measure	6
6	Perception of Leadership Team	Actions to address long standing frustrations of staff	5
7	Staff reluctance to change	Use demonstrator to build confidence	4
7	Over- promises made in the past	See above	7
6	Poor view of current communications	Install regular simple communications	3

Key relationship mapping

Whilst Force Field Analysis works with the broad views and perceptions of the organisation, Key Relationship Mapping can be used to assess critical individuals and the roles to which they are suited. This needs to be done by the Leadership Team.

1) Identify the people with the ability to have a strong positive or negative impact on the change process:

Who has power to help or hinder the change? This power might be formal authority,

a position of responsibility (e.g. an employee representative) or a strong position of influence.

Who has information that might help with the change? This information might be hard data or soft information e.g. a good understanding of the views of a particular staff group.

2) For each individual ask yourself whether you think they will benefit from the specifics of the change (i.e. be a winner) or whether they may lose out in any way.

3) Next ask yourself what the individual's perception might be if they knew the details of the change. The Japanese use Nemawashi in this process.

4) Actions should be determined based on the following guidelines:

Find opportunities to involve those who have information and power in the change process.

If any of these individuals will be losers in the process decide an approach for working with this person

Take every opportunity to turn key individuals from losers to winners.

Nemawashi

The Japanese technique "Nemawashi" addresses some of the same issues and is perhaps more prescriptive.

Nemawashi is the building of support for a project through communication and consensus. Widely used in Japan, the ideas are taught to anyone involved in planning change, which in most organisations is everyone.

The Japanese term Nemawashi comes from "to dig around the roots" in order to prepare a plant for transplant. The focus is to think about the change from the point of view of the individuals who are impacted. The material below is in an early translation of a Nemawashi checklist but conveys the essence of the ideas.

Checklist for Conducting Nemawashi:*

> 1) Are you depending only on formal logic? (Logic may not work.)
>
> 2) Aren't you trying to get things done based only upon official stances? (There are true, underlying intentions, which are rather more important.)
>
> 3) Has Nemawashi been sufficiently conducted with all persons concerned? (If even one person has been left out, it may cause problems.)
>
> 4) Have you considered the position and circumstances of the other party very well? (It will not work unless you put yourself in the other party's position.)
>
> 5) Haven't you taken lightly conventional practices or formalities? (You cannot be too careful of them.)
>
> 6) Have you fully consulted with the person or department which would be most affected as a result of implementation? (High-pressuring the weak can only cause troubles later on.)
>
> 7) Is the timing correct? (Too early or too late leads to failure.)
>
> 8) Is there no problem in notification? (Thinking that you have notified someone is not good enough. Be sure to confirm as well.)
>
> 9) Have you studied the scope of what you will do yourself, and what will require cooperation?
>
> 10) As a result of implementation, will any new problem arise?

> 'Monden, Yasuhiro (1998), Toyota Production System, An Integrated Approach to Just-In-Time, Third edition, Norcross, GA: Engineering & Management Press, ISBN 041283930X.

In conclusion, managing roadblocks is another critical leadership issue. All of these techniques will help identify problems and issues. Nemawashi also points the way to solutions.

It is worth noting:

> The most vocal opponents of change often become the most committed supporters if their views are heard.

> Managers, especially senior ones, are very good at playing the game. They may appear very supportive but be quite concerned or even disruptive behind the scenes.

> Middle managers often have considerable commitment, knowledge and influence, and this has a stabilising effect on the organisation. Unless they are involved in the change process they may fear loss of control and become a focus for resistance.

Communications for the change process

For many organisations internal communications is their "Bête noire". Leaders may feel that communication with staff is already superb, but recipients seldom feel communication is good enough. Embarking on a change programme provides an opportunity to review the existing communication processes and to introduce some best practice.

World-class organisations will have much of what follows in place but, even so benchmarking work will often reveal new ideas.

There have been many studies that test the effectiveness of organisations' communications. With few exceptions, people prefer to be given important information directly by the boss in an environment where they can ask questions. Best practice is a 4-way process:

Key

1. The information the Leadership Team wish to communicate.

2. The feedback relating to that information.

3. The issues, concerns, improvements, proposals etc. that employees wish to communicate.

4. The feedback relating to that information.

Each formal communication session should not only seek feedback on the presented material, but should also be seeking ideas and alternatives. When these are offered they will merit discussion and a response.

One company introduced "Rumour Boards", i.e. notice boards where staff can write the latest rumours. These were then used as part of formal communications, to dispel or confirm the rumours. **"NO SECRETS NO SURPRISES!"**

Many Task Forces have used "road shows". Instead of inviting employees to a conference room, they found that taking presentations to the work place, e.g. using a flip chart and portable stand, is a good way to engage staff, encourage questions and provide minimal disruption to the organisation's operations. At first glance this might seem disruptive but in small groups of 6 to 10 it works well.

Other ideas include:

- An "Open House" in the Task Force area.
- Photo boards with a résumé for participants.
- A regular newsletter with photographs of contributors.

Task Force Leaders often comment that half their day is taken up in communications - time well spent.

Analysis techniques

Improvement projects need Tools & Techniques that are:

- Quick to learn.
- Can be assimilated by all employees.
- Can be applied by a team.
- The team can use to train others.

Those listed below have been found to meet these criteria. They are effective and can be understood in a few minutes by employees at all levels of the organisation. The Task Force doesn't need to learn them all at once and some they may not need at all, but an overview will be useful during training:

- Brainstorming.
- SWOT analysis
- Input / output analysis.
- Process modelling.
- Process mapping.
- Flowcharting.
- Value analysis and value stream mapping.
- Pareto analysis
- Classification by RRS - runner repeater stranger.
- Cause and effect analysis.
- 5 Whys.
- Risk analysis and FMEA.

Together they allow a team to generate a shared view of how an organisation works, its priorities and effective ways to bring about change.

Brainstorming

The first technique is the best known, although it has often been abused through misuse.

Rules of Brain-storming:

1) The team should ideally number between 6 and 12.

2) Agree the topic or issue.

3) Each member in turn produces an idea or passes.

4) Each idea is recorded – preferably word for word.

5) The leader is not there to supply ideas. Their role is to assist the team to make best use of these rules.

6) No idea is too unlikely, too obvious or too stupid to be recorded.

7) Ideas are called for until everyone has finished.

8) Ideas must not be discussed until everyone has finished.

9) During subsequent discussions, only criticise the idea, never the person.

Without training and some discipline, brainstorming will not be effective. Most commonly, those who are assertive in the group will determine the outcomes and few new ideas will surface. Each of the rules is there for a reason, although initially your staff may feel they know better.

Here are some suggestions to make the training work effectively:

• Ask for a volunteer from the group to act as "scribe". This frees the trainer to concentrate on the group and what is being said. The "volunteer" can be changed regularly.

• Write down the issue being brainstormed so that it is visible to the whole team.

• Start the brainstorming with whoever is nearest, then work round the team in sequence. Make sure the scribe has a chance to contribute. Change the direction for the next issue.

• When an idea is suggested give the scribe time to record it before asking for the next idea.

• Make sure the "Rules" are followed, using humour if you can, but your authority if you must.

• Plan how you will have the team "refine" the list. If necessary take a team break while you do this. Refining the list usually involves agreeing to remove duplicates, grouping items (e.g. by cause or type), creating a "ranking" or priority view and checking whether the result is "a shared view" of the team.

• Plan how you or the group will take the results forward and agree that with them.

One helpful variation is where each team member writes down their ideas on 'post-its'. This can helps break communication barriers in groups who are not accustomed to "speaking out". It can also assist in grouping the ideas.

In syndicate groups try brainstorming with a 'fun' subject before going for the important issues.

SWOT analysis

S	Strengths
W	Weaknesses
O	Opportunities
T	Threats

SWOT analysis is a great way to get a team to focus on an issue. The issue can be wide ranging or focussed; the future of the organisation or the design of a process or a single contentious idea.

Brainstorming is often used in conjunction with SWOT analysis to ensure that all views are represented and is a good test of how well the team are using the technique.

Key steps:

1) Use a white-board or flip chart. Write down the topic for SWOT

2) Explain the technique to the team using a SWOT diagram

Strengths	Weaknesses
Opportunities	Threats

3)   Take each quadrant in turn, starting with Strengths and "brainstorm" the team views. It is important to begin with strengths as, depending on the topic, many groups are reluctant to admit weaknesses initially.

4)   Outputs can be ranked or prioritised and can guide further work. A simple ranking method is to give each team member three "votes" for issues raised in each quadrant. The combined votes of the team will give a clear view of priorities.

SWOT can encourage a team to create a realistic picture of business strengths, weaknesses, opportunities and threats that the team can then adopt as a shared view.

The organisation should be trying to build on its strengths, admit and then address its weaknesses, identify its opportunities and threats. Threats are usually external and opportunities can be internal or external. Opportunities which are matched by strengths can be exploited. Threats covered by a weakness reveal vulnerability.

Input / output analysis

Input/Output or "I/O" Analysis is another simple technique, but like brainstorming it requires some discipline to be effective. The steps below are simple but the sequence is important. Many teams are desperate to define the inputs before tackling the outputs:

1. Put the process in the box.

2. Brainstorm the outputs.

3. Brainstorm the inputs.

4. Refine the key outputs.

5. Refine the key inputs.

A simple training example is "Making a cup of Tea". Most teams can create and agree a simple picture of this process in 5 or 10 minutes.

Follow the steps with the group:

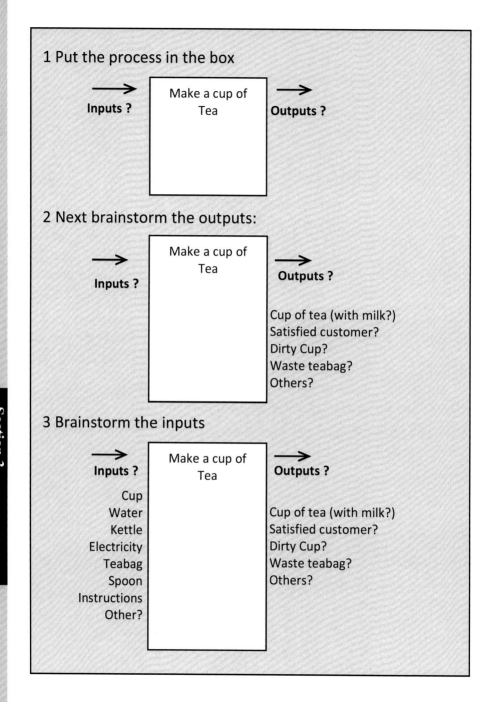

1 Put the process in the box

Inputs ? → | Make a cup of Tea | → Outputs ?

2 Next brainstorm the outputs:

Inputs ? → | Make a cup of Tea | → Outputs ?

Cup of tea (with milk?)
Satisfied customer?
Dirty Cup?
Waste teabag?
Others?

3 Brainstorm the inputs

Inputs ? → | Make a cup of Tea | → Outputs ?

Cup
Water
Kettle
Electricity
Teabag
Spoon
Instructions
Other?

Cup of tea (with milk?)
Satisfied customer?
Dirty Cup?
Waste teabag?
Others?

Steps 4 and 5 - "refine the inputs and outputs", will be simple in this example but the trainer should encourage a discussion about the assumptions which are made about the tea making process.

The technique can be used to generate a team view of almost anything. It is very useful for generating a top-level view of a project plan or a change program. The I/O diagram for a change program might look like:

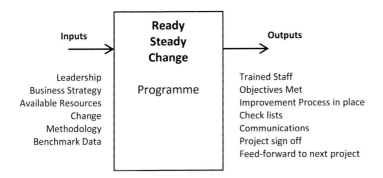

This high level view will need more detail to be useful. It can be displayed as a "Cascaded I/O Diagram", highlighting the key inputs and outputs for each step:

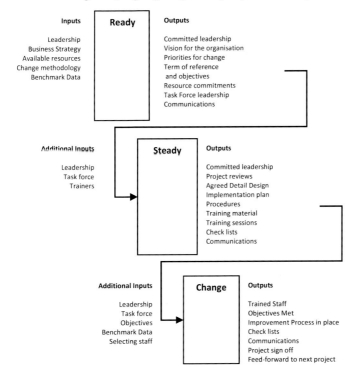

This type of cascading can help teams break a large task into manageable sections.

An Input/Output diagram can also be used to give a top-level view of the function of a department, business unit or a team. It is often used to help map processes where a cascaded version works well.

A departmental Input/Output analysis can provide a picture of what a department does, who its clients are and the resources consumed in supplying the service.

Basic Departmental I/O Template

Supplier	Input	Function	Output	Resource used	Customer
		Operational tasks			
		Housekeeping			
		Management			
		Training			
		Misc			

This analysis can be developed further. An estimate of time and cost of each activity provides a quantified view of the function. The resource used in the function can be checked. This can then be discussed, challenged and refined.

Example Departmental I/O analysis

Supplier	Input	ESTIMATING DEPT	Output	Customer	%
Manuf'g Eng	Standard	Review standards	Checked standard	Estimating	10%
Manuf'g Eng Production	Standard,'Look See' Manuf'g plans	Verify standards	Verified standard	Estimating	10%
Purchase Finance Estimating	Costs, standard Costs & O'heads Actual costs	Prepare estimate	Estimate	Contracts Dept	40%
Manuf'g Eng Production Prod'n Control Engineering Division	Request	Estimates for other functions	Estimate	Manuf'g Eng Production Prod'n Control Engineering Division	5%
Finance Division	Request (Bi annual)	Prepare budgets	Budget	Finance Division	2%
Finance Division	Request	Develop cost reduction proposals	Proposal	Finance Division	2%
Commercial	Request	Develop commercial systems	System	Commercial	10%
Manuf'g Eng	Eng Change	Change control	Change costing	Manuf'g Eng Finance	2%
Commercial/ Estimating	People	Training/Meetings and other	People	Commercial/ Estimating	16%

In this illustration the team has analysed the work of the estimating department, established the "customers" of the service and the proportion of the estimating department's work that is done for each activity. The Task Force used the information to propose a reorganisation based on process rather than function. The above analysis also helped assess the staffing and skills required in the new structure.

Process modelling

Much has been written on the subject of business models in general and process models in particular. Although this is not strictly a change management topic, an organisation should have a shared understanding of how it fits in the "value network" for its chosen market and the key processes which it uses to serve the customer. This model of the organisation not only aids an understanding of how things work, but also helps to develop options and opportunities to make effective change.

In our view, the most effective approach is to identify the top-level processes for the organisation and agree a visible model in the Michael Porter or the John Parnaby style.

A very common business model takes the form:

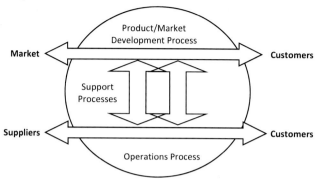

In this example two key processes serve the customer. The processes are depicted as arrows which are bi-directional because, although the products flow towards the customer, information flows in both directions.

The Product/Market development process, is the process used in the development of new products, or the modification of existing products. It also represents the process to develop new or existing market opportunities for existing or new products. Development processes are often extremely complex and analysis like "Runner Repeater Stranger" is very helpful in unpicking the complexity.

The Operations process is the process by which the product or service is delivered to the customer and it includes a number of sub-processes typically: Winning business, operations planning, material acquisition, supplier payment, manufacture, distribution, cash collection and bill payment.

Other processes exist to support these major processes. Examples include: Finance, HR, IT Support etc. One Task Force developed the model below for the basic processes within a polymer business:

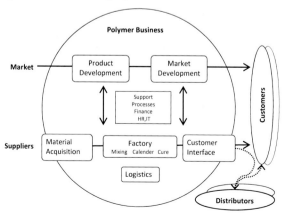

102

It is easy to extend this basic process model to represent the supply network for an organisation and also interrelationships in organisations which have decentralised business units with shared corporate services. Some examples of process models for different types of organisation follow.

A simplified supply network model

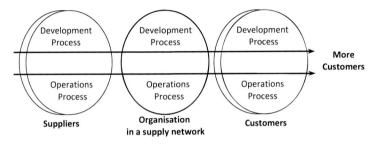

This type of model can help highlight the opportunities of working with key suppliers and customers for mutual benefit. It demonstrates opportunities to work together in product and market development as well as operations and logistics.

In some situations it helps to visualise opportunities to leapfrog competitors or to control the supply network by using technology.

A simplified Charity organisation model

The high level processes in charities are similar to other organisations, however there are differences which are useful to note.

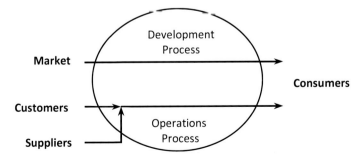

Simplified Charity organisation model

The recipients of the products and services of a charity are usually "consumers" rather than customers. Consumers receive and use the outputs of the charity but don't normally pay for them.

"Customers" provide cash or other valuables to charities but don't receive their services. Some charity customers do require feedback to demonstrate the satisfaction of consumers. Some don't want feedback, preferring to be reassured that the money is well spent and that charity administration costs are minimised.

Suppliers to charities are similar to those in other models, with the same opportunities for process integration and improvement.

The operation process will vary widely depending on the nature of the charity. The development process in a charity is likely to address both:

• Market development e.g. how to attract new groups of customers (cash providers) and how to meet their needs for feedback.

• Operations process development e.g. how to better address the needs of consumers.

A simplified Local Authority Model

Local authorities are more complex than many of the preceding organisations. The customer / supplier relationships which are the backbone of most commercial organisations are supplemented by relationships with electors, National Government, NHS, etc.

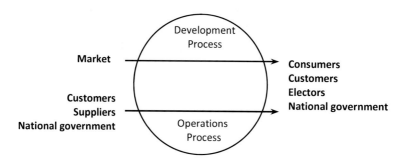

Simplified Local Authority model

Consumers include those receiving social services, roads and park services, school children, etc.

Customers who pay directly for services include "ratepayers" at one extreme and attendees at the local swimming pool at the other. If we were developing this model it might be useful to distinguish customers without choice ("tax payers") from the others. Electors may also be customers and will be consumers. National Government provides funds as well as regulation and expects targets to be met.

Despite the complexity, progress is being made in Local Authorities by identifying discrete parts of the operations process and using teams to generate simplification.

Hospital model

Attempting a process model of the National Health Service is well beyond the scope of this guide, but a simplified Hospital model has been included along with

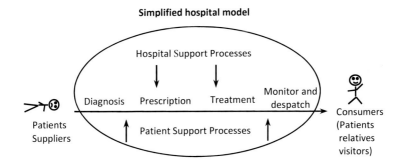

Simplified hospital model

a practical example.

Hospitals have been likened to repair and overhaul businesses and there are some common features. The basic process is shown above, with diagnosis and prescription, through treatment and hopefully to a successful discharge. In this model, patient support processes include many of the nursing functions as well as catering and cleaning.

The following process model which was prepared for the NHS trust (Acute). It shows additional detail and uses the language of the contributors.

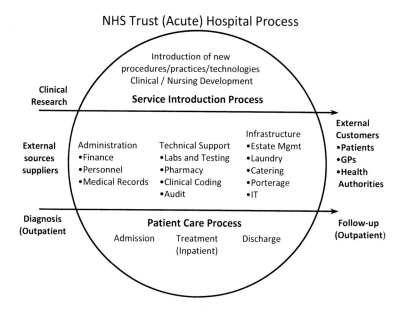

NHS Trust (Acute) Hospital Process

Clinical Research

Introduction of new procedures/practices/technologies
Clinical / Nursing Development

Service Introduction Process

External sources suppliers

Administration	Technical Support	Infrastructure
•Finance	•Labs and Testing	•Estate Mgmt
•Personnel	•Pharmacy	•Laundry
•Medical Records	•Clinical Coding	•Catering
	•Audit	•Porterage
		•IT

External Customers
•Patients
•GPs
•Health Authorities

Diagnosis (Outpatient

Patient Care Process

Admission   Treatment (Inpatient)   Discharge

Follow-up (Outpatient)

Organisations in this sector are increasingly using techniques like Runner Repeater Stranger to design operations processes that can treat patients effectively.

Process mapping

Process mapping techniques are vital to create visible representations of complex business processes. These representations are needed to analyse and then redesign the processes. The following notes describe some of the process mapping techniques and provide guidance on when they should be used.

The first step of process mapping is to identify the process or sub-process in the organisation which will be the target for analysis or redesign.

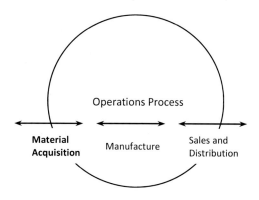

Operations Process

Material Acquisition   Manufacture   Sales and Distribution

I/O analysis is then used to develop a top-level view of the outputs of the process, which can subsequently be checked against current practice.

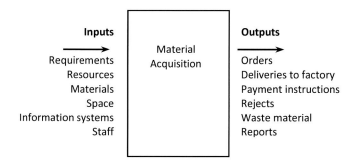

It is often effective to prepare a cascaded I/O at this stage to allow extra detail, but still at a high level.

The next step is process mapping using 'Post It' stickers to describe the activities in the process. This is a very effective way for a Task Force to generate an extra level of detail about a process or sub process. A quick picture, created by the team based on what they collectively know, often helps a shared understanding of a target process and can help focus further analytical work. Team members write a short description of important steps of the process on "Post its". These can be attached to a white board and moved around to get the right sequence.

Finally, problem areas, bottlenecks and opportunities for Runner/Repeater/Strangers Analysis can be highlighted.

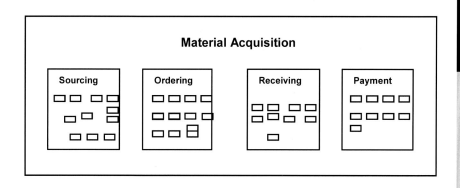

In the above example, the main sub processes might include:

- Receive demand from the customer or the factory.
- Plan material requirement.
- Order materials.
- Progress material orders.
- Receive materials from supplier.
- Receive and check paperwork (purchase orders to delivery notes).
- Check materials.
- Store materials.
- Move materials to factory.
- Pay invoices.
- Produce reports.

These processes and the activities within them need to be challenged:

- Do they add value?

- How can no added value work be avoided?

- Do world class organisations do it differently?

In world class automotive manufacture, most of the above processes have been eliminated. The supplier delivers direct to the production facility based on the factory plan or a "KANBAN" system. The customer calculates the payment due to the supplier. This is an automated process based on the number of vehicles produced. If the vehicle was produced, the supplier must have provided the appropriate component parts. This provides a major simplification and cost reduction for both the customer and supplier.

A continuous improvement group is unlikely to arrive at such a radical solution, but a Task Force may, particularly if they are allowed the opportunity to undertake external benchmarking.

When the process has been streamlined, the design of the organisation that will operate it can commence.

Flowcharting

This is among the longest established techniques for process mapping, however Task Forces should reserve the use of flowcharting for parts of the process where detailed information is really required.

At its simplest level, a block diagram can be used to represent process flow.

Material flow for a textile manufacturing process

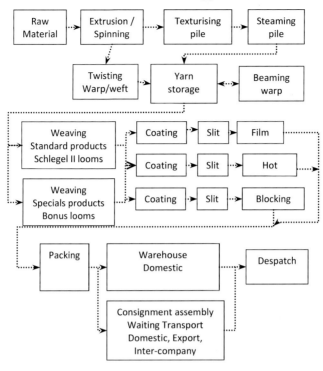

This type of block diagram schematic of a physical flow is invaluable to provide a shared view for a team. It can also be used for a high level view of information flow.

Information flows can also be charted using readily identified symbols. A number of conventions exist and can be accessed on the internet but these basic symbols are available in standard software packages and will serve the Task Force well:

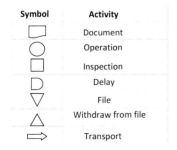

Symbol	Activity
	Document
	Operation
	Inspection
	Delay
	File
	Withdraw from file
	Transport

The concepts of "value added" (VA) and "no value added" (NVA) are also useful. The definitions of the terms are much debated but the concept is straightforward. A value added activity is an action which directly adds value for the customer e.g. in a hospital diagnosing the cause of an illness is value added.

A no value added activity is one which does not add value for the customer e.g. a support department checking another support department's work. The use of VA and NVA can help focus debate and waste reduction opportunities.

This is a summary of information flowcharting for a quotation for a new job:

Quotation process

Symbol	Activity	Number
▭	Document	9 and 2 accessed
◯	Operation	26
▢	Inspection	21
▷	Delay	14
▽	File	6
△	Withdraw from file	4
⇒	Transport	23

This quotation process example was prepared to illustrate the "need for change" and this type of charting is usually completed on detailed procedures as a preliminary to waste identification and process improvement. A quotation process which involves over 90 activities of which only 26 look value added is a candidate for change.

A data collection sheet is illustrated below:

Process Flow							Major						Date		
No a,b, et	Operatio						Description of activity	Qt	Di	D ay	Tim		Opportunity		Proposal
	O	▢	▽	D	⇨						H ou	Mi ns			
1															
2															
3															
4															
5															
6															
7															
8															
9															
1															
1															
1															
1															
1															
1															
1															
1															
1															
2															
				Tota											

This presentation format focuses on the movement of documents or online information between departments and helps identify potential "NVA" operations.

The following is an example of a customer enquiry process.

Customer enquiry process

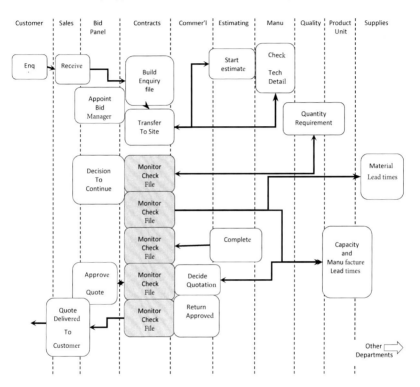

This example highlights the number of changes in ownership. Each change creates the opportunity for a delay and a communication problem. The shaded areas stood out as potential NVA; however the whole of the above process is fragmented and needs to be redesigned.

Value analysis and value stream mapping

It is beyond the scope of his guide to do more than mention the topics of "Value analysis "and "Value stream mapping".

Value analysis is a systematic approach to the redesign of products or processes through repeatedly asking whether cost or time can be eliminated for each component or at each stage. It was developed in manufacturing organisations but can also be applied elsewhere.

Value Stream Mapping is a related set of techniques used to analyze the flow of materials and information throughout an organisation. The technique was developed by Toyota, but the symbols used in value stream mapping are not standardised, except within organisations.

It is normal to prepare an "as is " value stream map showing, for example, information flow, product data (e.g. volumes or weights) and process data (e.g. process speeds wastage and delays or queues).

The process is assessed and redesigned using techniques like value analysis or other techniques referred to in this guide.

A future state value stream map is prepared to assist communication and implementation.

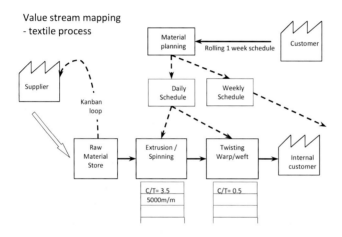

There is a risk that task forces will prepare over-complex value stream maps and get lost in the detail. It is important to focus detailed work on critical process at the appropriate time.

Pareto analysis

Pareto analysis is also known as the 80/20 rule and is similar to ABC analysis.

Pareto analysis may demonstrate that a disproportionate improvement can be achieved by ranking various causes of a problem and by concentrating on those solutions or items with the largest impact. The basic premise is that not all inputs have the same or even proportional impact on a given output.

Put more simply, Pareto can separate the vital few from the trivial many.

For example sales by product: 80% of sales arise from 20% of the product range; or defects by cause: 80% of defects result from 20% of possible causes.

In the following example, 80% of the organisations' spend on "component parts" arises from 20% of component types. A purchasing study to reduce input costs might do well to concentrate their efforts on that 20%.

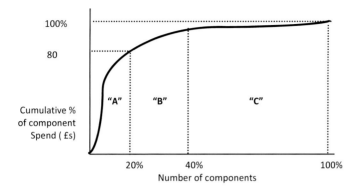

There is no guarantee that the Pareto effect will apply. The data must be collected and analysed. If it applies, its use can simplify and shorten the work to address problems or take advantage of opportunities. It is a method of classification that provides focus.

Classification by RRS - runners repeaters strangers

Runners Repeaters Strangers analysis is a separate but similar way of classifying events or items to improve processing. The event or item can be a physical product, a service or any other activity. The 80/20 rule described above may apply to these events, but RRS can be effective whatever the distribution.

The definitions are:

• A "Runner"; a frequent occurrence, the majority of events fall into this category.

• A "Repeater"; a regular occurrence.

• A "Stranger"; events which happen occasionally but which often have peculiarities which require special attention.

In the past, organisations (or processes) may have developed in a way where they could deal with all eventualities. Although this can provide great flexibility in dealing with a range of changing customer requirements, it may overcomplicate the processing of routine tasks and not provide the most competitive process to deliver value.

If we take as an example a family of manufactured components, they might be classified to take account of their complexity and frequency of manufacture:

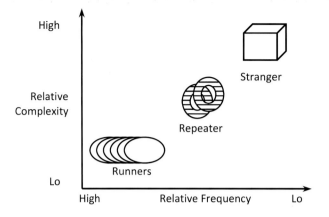

Has the simplest process been designed for each classification?

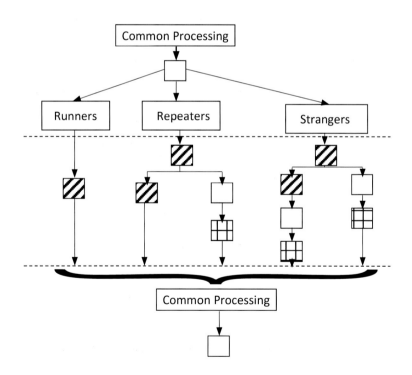

114

Runners, repeaters and strangers do not have to be physical products but they can be processes, events or actions.

Process	Runner	Repeater	Stranger
Customer Ordering	Standard Product With a regular customer	Standard product with a new customer or a slightly modified product with a regular customer	A bespoke product
Material acquisition	Established material with a regular supplier for a regular amount	Repeat material but with low or irregular demand	A one-off purchase
Design change request	Request not affecting the form, fit or function of the product or system	Request which will require significant input and analysis	A redesign of the product is required

The following example shows the technique applied to product change requests:

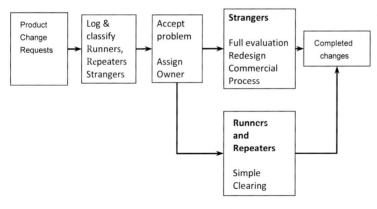

The simple process has a much shorter lead-time for the majority of the change requests.

The process redesign work will ensure that

- The right team of staff
- With the right skills
- With the right equipment
- With the right training and operating procedures

are drawn together to run the process.

Within a training environment, runners, repeaters and strangers can be identified in one or two different situations: e.g. "medical conditions" or "passport enquiries". Also try using the technique using an event relevant to the organisation.

RRS has yielded spectacular benefits in a number of industries. It was initially applied in the introduction of cellular manufacture by Lucas Engineering and Systems Ltd. Historically a component manufacturing plant was laid out by function, mills drills presses, etc. A machine shop in this layout could manufacture almost anything, but the processing paths were long and convoluted. A cellular design which grouped plant appropriately, improved quality, reduced inventory, reduced lead-time and reduced cost.

The same concepts can now be seen working in the NHS. A number of medical conditions have been identified as runners e.g. hip replacement, cornea replacement, etc., and specialist units have been established throughout the country. Rare conditions are increasingly being dealt with in specialist units.

Cause and effect analysis

This is another technique that works well in a team environment. When a critical problem is identified it is highlighted on a Cause and Effect diagram (also known as a fishbone diagram).

The possible key causes are identified and grouped on the limbs of the diagram. Data is then collected to assess the significance of these causes. In the classic version, the groupings used are People Machines, Methods and Materials.

The possible causes can be brainstormed and written on Post-it Notes to populate a cause and effect diagram.

Example of an information problem:

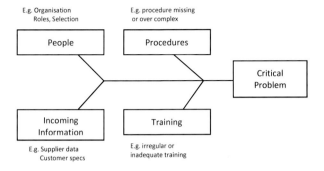

The cause/effect diagram can also be cascaded:

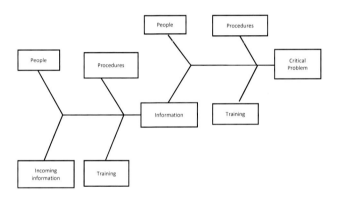

This type of cascading can be repeated as often as necessary.

Once the generic Cause and Effect diagram has been developed, data should be collected and analysed to confirm the most likely cause.

5 Whys

The 5 Whys technique* is related to Cause and Effect analysis to arrive at root causes of a problem by asking the question "Why" repeatedly. Solutions or mitigations should then be developed.

*Source Monden, Yasuhiro (1998), Toyota Production System, An Integrated Approach to Just-In-Time, Third edition, Norcross, GA: Engineering & Management Press, ISBN 0-412-83930-X

For example:

My car won't start. (the problem):

- Why? - The battery is flat.
- Why? - The alternator isn't charging.
- Why? - The fan belt is loose.
- Why? - The car wasn't serviced.
- Why? - I was trying to save money.

When learning this technique, try asking a training group to suggest a common work-related problem and then try the repeated "Why" technique.

This technique, like brainstorming, needs to be undertaken with some discipline if it is to be effective.

Risk analysis and FMEA

Organisations cannot make changes without taking risks. Much of the work done by a Task Force is to minimise the risk of failure. Leaders will often make a judgment of the level of risk associated with a particular project, but a formal risk assessment will provide a more objective outcome. Organisations usually have documented processes for risk assessment which can be used or adapted. SWOT analysis provides a useful tool to help an individual or a team to identify threats. For this purpose it may be helpful to categorise them, e.g. human, technical, operational, etc.

Once a risk has been identified:

1) Estimate the probability of the risk occurring.

2) Quantify the impact of the risk if it occurs.

3) Propose an action to reduce the probability of it occurring (mitigation).

4) Propose and action to lessen the impact if it does occur (contingency).

Risk is sometimes defined as the perceived extent of possible losses. Different people will have different views of the impact of a particular risk – what may be a small risk for one person may be unacceptable for someone else.

One way of assessing risk is to calculate a value for it:

Risk = probability of event x cost of its impact.

A series of alternative scenarios can be assessed using the same criteria to create comparisons of risk and benefit.

Failure Mode and Effect analysis is a much used tool for assessing risk and has been used extensively in the automotive sector (e.g. Ford Motor Company) for evaluating potential design and manufacturing process failures.

This table shows how possible failures are assessed:

1	Process Component or Product	E.g. Piston	E.g. Seal
2	Purpose	Braking	TBC
3	Failure Cause	Cracking	TBC
4	Failure Cost £	£1m	TBC
5	Ease of Detection 1 easy - 5 difficult	4	TBC
6	Severity of Effect 1 low - 5 high	5	TBC
7	Probability of Failure 1 to 100	1	TBC
8	Risk Score = Row5 x R6 x R7	20	TBC

The resultant score ranking can help identify the processes or components and failure modes which are most in need of attention. A variant of this will also be used for health and safety assessment prior to potential changes to physical layouts, etc.

Some practioners highlight that opportunities are "positive risks" and often change projects identify opportunities to increase the benefits e.g. speaking with potential or lost customers during the analysis phase may reveal opportunities to win new business.

5 Ss for workplace organisation

This technique is credited to Hiroyuki Hirano, author of "5 Pillars of the Visual Workplace ". It provides a discipline and framework for improving the housekeeping and operation of the workplace. It works well in teams when coupled with brainstorming the potential actions that might be taken. The 5 Ss give 5 areas of opportunity for improvement:

- Seiri (Organisation - sort through and sort out)
- Seiton (Orderliness - set things in order, set limits, share information)
- Seiso (Cleanliness - shine equipment, tools, the whole workplace
- Seiketsu (Neatness)
- Shitsuke (Discipline stick to the rules)

An English language version is CANDO which is perhaps more memorable.

- Clean
- Arrangement
- Neatness
- Discipline
- Order

Whichever acronym you choose, these basics are critical to team performance and improvement. There is no better time to establish this good practice than when setting up a new workplace team.

Team measures of performance

Measures of performance are critical in any organisation, however over-complex measures or overambitious targets can inhibit performance improvement. In a well-designed organisation the teams will be structured around major processes and will feel responsible for both the operation of the process and for its improvement. This allows for straightforward performance measurement. At team level, a simple balanced set of measures might address:

- Cost - e.g. cost of waste, time or materials.
- Quality - e.g. performance to specification of the product or service that the process delivers.
- Delivery - e.g. adherence to schedule, lead-time reduction.

In a process redesign project the following guidelines should be followed when measures are designed and target levels set for the operational team:

- Measures should be agreed between the team and the Task Force.
- The target levels should be agreed by all.

Performance against target should be measured and displayed. If possible automatically and in real time. Otherwise team members should be responsible for the monitoring and displaying their own measurements. Records can be kept, should audits be required.

Measures should be visible. Graphs are good because they show trends and history:

- Measures should be unambiguous. They should encourage the team to improve performance.

- Team measures of performance should not be a basis for payment. This is sometimes a controversial issue, but bonus payments based, for example, on output have a poor track record, either in providing real motivation or in providing customer service.

If measures of performance are set up effectively, the team will feel real ownership. They will also feel pride in meeting targets. One executive observed, "I want the team to leave for the weekend feeling like winners not losers!"

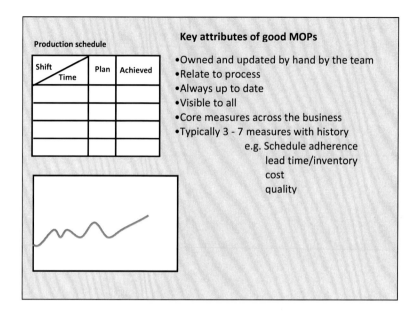

Visible MOPs also help visiting staff, customers and suppliers to quickly appreciate the focus of the team and its performance level. Some organisations pride themselves in displaying information in a form that overseas visitors can understand without asking for translations or explanations.

Team training 5*

Staff training is fundamental to effective implementation and operation of changed processes. Team based operations rely on staff flexibility. Not all staff on a team need to be capable of undertaking all the team tasks, but adequate cover for peak periods, holidays, absence, etc. is needed. The use of a training matrix which is displayed in the team area provides the base for a very effective personnel development process.

5 ☆ Photo / Team Members	Key Team Activities						
	Daily Planning	House keeping	Complaints Process	Quotation Process	Order Processing	Consumable Supply	Etc ..
(photo) Fred Smith (Team Leader)	☆☆☆☆☆	☆☆☆☆☆	★	☆☆☆		☆☆☆☆☆	
(photo) Bill Jones	★	☆ ☆	☆☆☆	☆☆☆	☆	☆	
(photo) Jane Robinson	☆☆☆☆☆	☆☆☆	☆☆ ★	☆☆☆☆	☆	☆	
(photo) (photo)							
Typically 5 – 10 team members — Total ☆☆☆+							

The matrix comprises a number of columns which highlight the core skills needed to operate the module. Each team member is assigned a row, and their capability in each core skill is assessed. In some safety critical industries this can be a very formal process with testing and regular reviews. The assessment grades up to 5 stars, give the technique its name.

The "total" is the number of staff at "3 star" and above because this provides a quick view of the level of skills coverage.

The Team leader should ensure that:

1) Each team activity has enough people at 3 stars and above i.e. people to do the job.

2) There is at least one team member with a 5 star rating for each activity. This makes the team self-sustaining as they will be able to self-train.

3) Regularly review the training needs and plans ensuring team flexibility and growth of the individual.

The most common 5 star definitions are:

☆   Basic Health and safety training only

☆☆   Basic Skills training completed satisfactorily

☆☆☆   Experienced

☆☆☆☆   Authorised to self-inspect

☆☆☆☆☆   Trained to train others

★   Means that training is planned next month

ILU is also widely used as an alternative rating system. I - Trained, L - Experienced, U - able to self-inspect and a closed box able to train others.

In both cases it must be emphasized that the systems rate competence for a particular capability. It does not rate the competence of the person.

The transition curve

Leaders can be more effective if they understand how people respond to change. There are many models that describe how someone's feelings and motivations alter during the process of change. Most of these have their origin with some pioneering work by Elizabeth Kubler-Ross on the emotions of bereavement.

For change management we find the Transition Curve* to be the most helpful, as it explains the stages involved in seeing a change through from the start to its successful completion.

Source:

Transitions : positive change in your life & work. Author: Barrie Hopson; Mike Scally Publisher: Amsterdam ; San Diego : Pfeiffer & Co., ©1993.

The

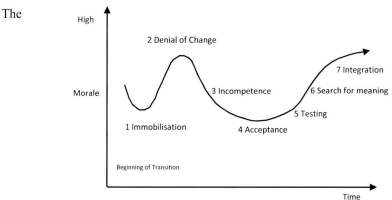

Transition Curve describes 7 stages:

Stage 1: Immobilisation - occurs when the change first bites and is accompanied by a loss of morale due to being shocked or overwhelmed. Typical comments – why do we need to change; will there be redundancies?

Stage 2: Denial of Change – starts with questioning and leads to a "denial" of the need to change. This stage is characterised by an improvement in morale. Typical comments – we have seen all this before; nothing will happen because nothing ever does; I am ok, it's the others.

Stage 3: Incompetence - is a loss of morale that occurs as it becomes clear that the change will not go away and the person feels unable to cope. This stage is often characterised by frustration. Typical comments – I'm confused; what is it that is required; why don't they just get on with it, after all they have already decided what they are going to do.

Stage 4: Acceptance of Reality - is the stage at which people individually decide to accept the change and to let go of the past. This is usually when people are at their lowest point. Typical comments – let's get on with it; what's next; am I going to receive help in making this change?

Stage 5: Testing - is the stage at which people begin to test what the change will mean to them in practice and is characterised by improving morale. Typical comment – "could it work like this? "

Stage 6: Search for Meaning - is when someone begins to understand for themselves what the change means and the stage is often characterised by discussing what it means with colleagues. Typical comments – now I get it; how are you handling this; could we work together?

Stage 7: Integration - is when the new behaviours are embedded in to old patterns of work. Typical comment: – "I believe this will work".

People gain a better understanding of these stages if they can relate to a significant event in their own lives. They are often very personal in nature:

- Death of a spouse
- Loss of job
- Divorce

These emotions can also be expressed in apparently more positive events:

- Getting married
- Moving job or home

There is evidence that all such events can trigger a transition curve response. When multiple events occur over a short period of time, they can be cumulative and have a greater impact.

In a domestic context, people rely on support from friends and relatives. Different organisations have a very varied approach in offering support to their staff during change.

The Ready Steady Change methodology provides a framework which can help individuals deal with the change in their organisation. The aim is to minimise the impact of change on the individual by reducing the depth of the trough and also its duration.

The transition curve below was prepared by the Sponsor and the Task Force in one industrial business. It highlights some of their actions taken before, during and after implementation.

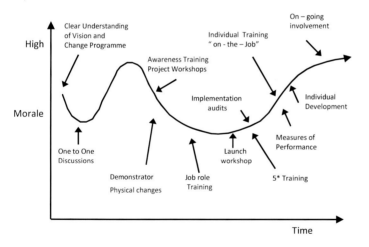

Many of these actions help address the fear of the unknown and assess the attitude of the staff involved.

Implementation audit

This audit framework was used by a team who were implementing major change in an aerospace business. It is followed by some detailed questions which are relevant to many implementations. However this type of list needs to be recreated for each situation or at least challenged and regenerated each time.

XYZ Organisation	Implementation Audit							
Auditor	Key :	1. Disagree Totally 2. Agree Partially 3. Agree Mostly 4. Agree Totally						
AUDIT POINT	Score						Date.	
	1	2	3	4	Comment or Action	Who	When
Project Set-Up								
1								

Some of the detailed questions which were addressed in the above framework
are set out below (the rows in the table).

Project Set-Up	
1	Terms of Reference exist and clearly state: project scope, target objectives, deliverables, timescale, approach, team composition including part-time members and roles, project review and control mechanism.
2	Task Force adequately resourced and trained in Process Redesign Methodology.
3	Adequate facilities provided including Task Force office, whiteboards, telephone, personal computer and software, and access to secretarial support, conference room and photocopier.
4	Project Owner appointed, Steering Group formed and roles clarified.
5	Project budget agreed.

Project Plans	
6	Top level project plan and work-package plans exist, are up to date and are visibly displayed in Task Force office.
7	Project Plans indicate resource availability, and milestones, and have been signed-off by the Task Force Leader
8	Hazard criteria agreed with steering group and adhered to.

	Project Control
9	Daily Task Force meetings exist, are attended by all full time members and visible daily action list updated, indicating by whom and by when tasks are to be completed.
10	Weekly control meetings with project owner exist, are attended by all the full-time members and minutes and actions from the meeting along with an updated copy of the project plan are distributed to all members of the steering group.
11	Monthly steering group review meetings exist, have dates and times fixed for the next 3 meetings, are attended by at least two thirds of the steering group, and have minutes and actions produced and distributed to the steering group.
12	A single project file exists containing copies of the project terms of reference, project plan, weekly control meeting minutes and actions, monthly steering group review presentations, and actions, design documentation and other background information.
	Task Force Teamwork
13	The skills and attributes of the individual Task Force members is understood and evidence that best use is being made of the team's strengths.
14	Evidence that out of work teambuilding activities are taking place.
	Task Force Support
15	Adequate day to day engineer support, periodic technical management and other specialist support is provided.
16	The project owner and steering group is providing adequate support.
	Communication
17	A communication plan exists, a monthly newsletter is produced and briefing given to the affected areas following the monthly steering group review.
18	Evidence exists that those likely to be affected by the project at least understand the objectives of the project.
	Concept Design Phase
19	The business strategy for the next 1--5 years is understood in terms of products, markets and customers.
20	The sales forecast and degree of confidence for the next 1--2 years is understood.
21	The immediate customer requirements in terms of delivery, price and quality performance is understood.
22	The current manufacturing performance w.r.t. the project objectives of delivery, lead time, stock turn and quality is understood.

23	Past and on-going manufacturing improvement initiatives are understood, incorporated and/or adjusted w.r.t. the project.
24	The prime causes of manufacturing failure to achieve the project objectives are understood and confirmation of the level of improvements expected from the project given.
25	The current organisation structure, job roles, and number of people in manufacturing and responsibilities understood.
26	The module/cell definition methodology is understood and at least 3 options considered with associated strengths and weaknesses analysis.
27	The preferred module/cell definition has been agreed by the steering group.
28	An organization structure to support the module/cell definition indicating main roles and estimated number of people required has also been agreed.
29	A runners, repeaters, strangers analysis on component and product demand has been completed to give some indication of the likely material control system required.
30	Quick hits have been highlighted, agreed and actioned by the steering group.

Detail Design Phase - Module/Cell Sizing

32	80%+ of demand has been used in the steady state sizing of the cells and capacity analysis carried out to determine the loading on bottleneck machines, the exact plant and equipment requirement and the exact number of operators required.
33	The key variables have been determined e.g. demand ± 20% key machine capability/reliability, and dynamic analysis carried out to assess the effect of the variables.
34	Actions to eliminate or lessen the variables have been taken.
35	A document has been produced of the definitive cell definition, indicating products, sub-assemblies and components, exact plant and equipment requirements and exact number of operators required.
36	The definitive cell definition has been checked by manufacturing personnel and accepted by the steering group.

People Issues

| 37 | A detailed Job Definition has been produced for each key role, and "bottom up" assessment made of module and cell tasks, the size of these tasks, who should perform the tasks and hence how many support roles are required. |
| 38 | A training framework has been developed e.g. 5 star and a skills audit carried out on the likely cell and module personnel. |

39	Generic training plans have been developed for the module leader, cell leader, module and cell support roles, and operators.
40	The existing payment system and any other terms and conditions issues likely to affect the achievement of the project objectives are understood.
41	The selection procedure for module and cell personnel has been agreed with the steering group.

Physical Layout and Environment

46	At least 3 module/cell layout options have been considered, with associated strengths and weaknesses and cost benefit statement.
47	The preferred option has been agreed by the steering group.
48	Best practice ideas have been incorporated into the cell layout and the personnel affected have been involved in detail design.
49	Each cell incorporates an operator rest area, meeting area with MOPs / Problem board and cell leader/support area.
50	Each cell incorporates specific areas for tools, jigs and fixtures and drawing storage, quality control equipment and packaging.
51	Each module/cell is identified with overhead signs, use of colour, floor lines and/or physical barriers, and a clear entrance and exit gateway.
52	Consideration has been given to Health and Safety and other environmental issues such as heating, light, and pollution from noise and fumes.
53	Material handling requirements have been specified, including racking, containers, trolleys, and lifting equipment.
54	Space has been set aside for anticipated expansion/new/replacement plant and equipment.
55	A document has been produced of the physical layout and environment proposals, costed and agreed by steering group.

Implementation Phase

56	An implementation project manager has been appointed and implementation team named, with clear definition of roles and responsibilities.
57	An implementation plan indicating activities, owners and due dates, is visible, up to date and acceptable by the steering group.

58	An implementation FMEA (Failure Mode and Effect Analysis) has been completed to help identify potential high risk areas.
59	Hazard criteria and escalation procedure have been agreed with the steering group.
60	Control meetings are occurring as per the Task Force terms of reference.
61	Account has been taken in the production schedule of the disruption to production during reconstruction, cell operator training, and cell commissioning.

Many of the implementation audit questions can be repeated during operational audits which are arranged post-implementation.

Appendix 1 Colleagues who have developed or used the methodology

We would like to acknowledge the contribution of the hundreds of managers and staff who have worked in Task Forces across the world. The following list is only a fraction of those involved. Our apologies for the many omissions.

Pankaj Acharya
Rob Aston
Phil Baker
Alistair Barr
Mark Baxter
Neil Bentley
Alison Biddulph
Roy Billingham
Keith Blacker
Angela Bowland
Edmund Bradford
Julie Brophie
Annette Brown
Phil Bulimore
Martin Butler
Caroline Casey
Daniel Churton
Julian Clarke
Rupert Connolly
Judith Cooper
John Cottrell
Phil Crossland
Steve Croxall
John Davies
Pauline Deacon
John Detheridge
Sajid Ditta

Nick Andrews
Sid Bains
Douglas Balfour
Sarah Bavester
David Beazley
Chris Best
Nicky Billingham
David Bird
Phil Boreland
Catherine Bowser
Martin Brooks
Simon Buesnel
John Burgess
Mike Carey
Dick Chase
Jeff Clark
Nick Condon
Chris Cookson
Allan Copper
Norma Craven
Chris Crow
Mike Dale
Roy Davis
Dave Dee
Richard Dew
Peter Dobbs

Jane Dodd
Richard Dovey
Peter Drummond
Jayne Eagles
Scott Edwards
Chris Evans
Robin Farey
Dave Farrow
Gavin Fielden
Carl Flatley
Mike Gardiner
John Golding
Ian Grimsley
Phil Gwynne
Elaine Hailes
Alec Halliwell
Matt Hancocks
Tim Hart
Mark Henley
Allan Hill
Graham Hird
Mark Hixon
Ken Hope
David Jensen
Ninder Johal
David Johnson
Peter Johnson
Dave Jones
Simon Jones
Uzam Khan
Brian Kinch
Chris Lattimer
Andrew Layton
Phil Lewis

Andrew Donald
Lorraine Dowd
Rosemary Dutfield
Jens Ebbesen
John Entwistle
Jill Evans
Ian Farnworth
Jack Ferguson
Stuart Fisher
Dave Friday
John Garside
Deborah Gold
Stuart Grant
Jose Guzman-Bello
Peter Gygax
Mike Hall
John Halton
Steve Harrington
Colin Hayward
Graham Henman
Tas Hind
Sharon Hirsh
Andrew Hollingshead
Paul Hopkins
Caroline Horne
Alan Hyman
Richard Le Jeune
Mark Johnson
Colin Jones
Martin Jones
Neil Kendrick
Sarah Kilroy
Richard Lane
Nicolette Lawson
Mike Lenton
Morcom Lunt

Archie MacPherson
Sue Marland
Simon Mason
Chris Merryman
James Miller
Arthur Mitchell
Duncan Moffat
Mel Mula
Elizabeth Naylor
Paul Newman
Chris Owen
Hugh Oxenham
Manesh Pandya
Simon Parker
John Paul
Robin Peters
Andrew Powell
Pete Prendville
Debbie Ralph
John Riley
James Rock
April Rose
Jitesh Samini
Allan Schofield
Mark Sealy
Nasir Shah
Peter Shephard
Kate Silvester
Pav Singh
Rachel Smith - Chopra
Richard Smyth
Tom Spink
Ted Stiles
Divakar Tailor
Richard Taylor
Mike Thacker

Sue Maddox
Ian Marshall
Mario Mergulhao
Brian Miles
Praful Mistry
Innes Mitchell
Will Muddyman
Graham Napier
Graham Newcombe
Gill Oborne
Jenny Owston
Subash Panchal
Allan Parker
Nicholas Parnaby
Julian Peck
Martin Poulsen
Pat Poynton
Tony Putsman
Bill Renwick
Andy Roberts
Dave Roden
Roger Salmon
Trish Scanlon
Paul Scott
Peter Seddon
Ian Shaw
Sue Sheward
Arthur Sinclair
Mike Slinger
Tony Smith
Brian Spanswick
Peter Stevens
Graham Stubbs
Martin Tarrent
Karen Weymouth
Steve Thomas

Ian Tidmarsh Jim Tizzard
Andrew Tobias Nigel Topping
John Tudor Andy Tune
Duncan Varnes Mark Vaux
Peter Vince Jonathan Wainwright
James Walker Sean Walsh
Andy Ward Stuart Wardle
Diane Waring Cathy Weatherburn
Gail Whitaker Jane Whitehurst
Maryjoy White Elwyn Williams
Geoff Williams Stephanie Williams
Iain Wasson Tim Williams
Ewan Wilson Dudley Wood
Mike Wyatt Uday Yadav
Peter Yates James Yearsley
Rob Yearsley Joanne Young

Finally we also acknowledge the contribution of Professor Dennis Towell and Professor Ashok Kochhar - many thanks.

Appendix 2 About the authors

Ian White

Ian's career includes experience as a business development director with Lucas Industries, CSC and UniPoly. He now provides clients with consultancy, mentoring and executive development support.

Andrew Kearns

Andrew has extensive change management and operations management experience with Lucas Industries, CSC, Caradon and Novar. He now works as an interim manager / management consultant. His interests include business transformation and practical approaches to change management.